MW00931540

Sheer Determination

Swimming Upstream
in a Downstream World

Keiko Kay Hirai

Copyright © 2017 Keiko Kay Hirai

All rights reserved.

Sheer Determination is a work of creative non-fiction.
The events are portrayed to the best of the author's memory.
While all of the stories in this book are true, some names and identifying
details have been changed to protect the privacy of the people involved.

CONTENTS

MESSAGE TO READERS

This book is interactive! I am thrilled to show you how to bring it to life. All the QR (Quick Response) codes throughout the book can be scanned with your Smartphone or iPad to watch the videos that were created especially for you.

How to Scan the QR Codes in This Book

Step 1: Download a *free* QR Code Reader onto your smartphone by searching the App Store. I selected the Kaywa Reader because it is free of advertisements.

Step 2: Tap the app once it has downloaded to your phone; this will open up the Reader. Tap again, and your camera will appear to be on. Hover over the code you wish to scan, and the camera will automatically take a picture of the QR code; then your phone will be directed to the respective web page on **KeikoKayHirai.com** that contains each video message.

Enjoy!

INVITATION TO READERS

I invite you to visit the following links to download your three free gifts:

Gift #1
12 Small Steps for Developing Strong Relationships

http://keikokayhirai.com/smallsteps

Gift #2
How to Find your Hidden Gifts

http://keikokayhirai.com/hiddengifts

Gift #3
12 Steps for Writing Your Memoir (and why you should do it)

http://keikokayhirai.com/12steps

FOREWORD

I have spent the last forty years building my socially-responsible business. During this time, many people have asked me the question, "What is the single most important thing you have done to build your successful business?"

My response usually goes something like this... Most of us work hard to make good things happen. We work to sharpen our skills. We put in long hours. We put ourselves out there and do our best to serve others. Perhaps most importantly, we try to see the good in the world. Yet, it is easy to forget the core values that lie deep within us, waiting to be awakened. It is essential to dig deep and uncover those values. If we don't make that effort, there is no passion, joy, or purposeful direction to our lives and we end up feeling lost or unfulfilled.

In this book, I share my ideas on how to awaken your passion, build your business, change the world, and love your life. When, not if, you fall, you will eventually pick yourself up, move forward, and become a wiser and stronger person.

I hope that reading about the fortunate and not-so-fortunate paths that I have taken to build my salon business will ignite your imagination and help you to see life in a whole new way. Try viewing events and outcomes not as they currently are, but in terms of what they could become. Realize, too, that it is not the things we do that are important; what matters most is the passion that drives us to do the things we do. Each chapter of this book provides life lessons that I learned through my journey as a business owner. I hope my life story will inspire you to take the necessary steps toward creating joy, fulfillment, and success in your life – both personally and professionally. One thing I know for sure. When I do something that makes a difference in someone's life, I fall into a blissful sleep at night. Knowing that I've played an important part in creating a win for my employees, customers, and the world is what brings meaning and purpose to my life. My wish is that you, too, can find the joy in helping others.

WATCH MY VIDEO:

Introduction – Welcome Message

http://keikokayhirai.com/sheer-determination-introduction-welcome-message/

CHAPTER 1:

I HATE MY HAIR!

I was sixteen years old and struggling to fit into American life. After being a star pupil in Japan, I had spent the last five years labeled "the dumb, Japanese girl" at Garfield High School in Seattle. The problem? My language was limited and I had no idea who I was. All I wanted was to fit in with my peers and have a sense of belonging in my new homeland.

One thing always caught my attention while I was in school. The popular girls spent a lot of time talking about their hair as they walked through the hallways between classes.

"Wow, Elsa, you have a new do! Looks nice!" exclaimed Janie. "Thank you. I just had it done yesterday!" Elsa beamed, as her curls bounced around her face. "I went to Mr. Murray's salon in the Schaffer Building in downtown Seattle. He's a bit pricey, but it was completely worth it. You should go!"

I was so tired of being an outsider, the girl who everyone thought of as an FOB – "Fresh Off the Boat" from Japan. When I spoke, I was constantly asked to repeat myself. For example, I would

3

get condescending comments like, "What did you just say? If you're trying to say "resting," that's *not* how it is pronounced! It's *not* "lest-ing," it's "resting."

Was I *really* that different? I must have been because I couldn't escape the almost daily reminders. It made me so self-conscious that a lot of times, during group conversations, I didn't say anything at all. I'm sure the other students thought I was stuck-up and not very friendly.

One day, I made up my mind to get my hair done by Mr. Murray, just like all the popular girls. Determined to see it through, I gathered all of the money that I had saved from babysitting and picking strawberries over the summer – a whopping $35. Money in hand, I jumped on a bus to downtown Seattle. The bus ride to the Schaffer Building felt endless, but I was vibrating with excitement after I arrived and rode the elevator up to Mr. Murray's fifth floor salon. My hope was that I would come back to school and the "in crowd" would finally see someone who looked more like them – not simply a girl from Japan.

When I walked through the entrance of the salon, there was no one at the front desk. Instead, I was greeted by the strong scent of a permanent wave solution. In awkward silence, I sat in one of the three chairs and waited impatiently for something to happen.

Finally, a young girl appeared and escorted me to the shampoo area. I happily settled my head against the shampoo bowl and felt a little better, only to have a few splashes of lukewarm water touch my scalp. With my hair barely wet, the stylist applied cold shampoo and began sliding her fingers through my hair and scalp. I thought to myself, "This can't be right."

I stayed very still, waiting for the girl to begin a more vigorous scrubbing of my scalp. It never happened. Instead, I realized the shampoo was abruptly over when she wrapped a towel around my

4

head and asked me to follow her to Mr. Murray's styling chair.

"What?" I wanted to say, "That didn't feel like you did anything. Shouldn't you keep shampooing?" But, I was too timid to say that to a person who was working at such an upscale salon.

The assistant, without saying a word, walked me over to an empty styling chair and motioned for me to sit down. Her stoic facial expression made me feel uncomfortable and unwanted. As I sat down and waited, staring at my round face wrapped with a towel in the large, square wall mirror, I wanted to hide.

From the corner of my eye, I could see a man tending to a blond-haired client a few chairs away from me and assumed that it was Mr. Murray. As he finished combing her hair and fussing over her long curls, he grabbed a spray can with one hand and with a waving motion, swiftly engulfed the woman's head in a shroud of mist.

"Oh, my gosh," I thought, "He is cementing her hairdo in place!"

To my surprise, however, Mr. Murray whipped off the lady's cape with a flourish and the overjoyed client jumped up from the chair to give him a big hug!

"I love what you did for me. Thank you!" she exclaimed.

Mr. Murray grinned and gushed, "Isn't it great? You look so beautiful!"

The next thing I knew, Mr. Murray was rushing towards me dressed in his French artist's black turtleneck and boxy trousers. With soft, brown hair and deep, sparkling eyes, he exuded charisma. It was easy to see why he was so popular among so many of the girls at school.

He quickly whipped the towel off my head and shook my hair out. "Okay, I can see that you have lots of hair. I will give you a very nice cut and style," he promised.

Mr. Murray swiveled the chair away from the mirror and immediately began cutting and snipping away at my hair. I was so excited to see the "new" me that I barely noticed that he hadn't asked me how I wanted my hair cut or what I expected for the finished result. After thinking about it for a moment, I reasoned that since I was paying such a high price for the haircut, I should just let him use his best judgment to decide what was good for me.

He worked quickly, like he was in a hurry, and was soon drying my hair and settling it into place with his fingers. Then, without a word of warning, I was sitting in a cloud of toxic, smelly fumes – just like his other client. Similarly, my cape was drawn away with a smug smile from Mr. Murray and I was quickly turned to face the mirror. I was beside myself and had no idea what to say. For sure, I was transformed – but like this? My bangs had been cut into a horseshoe shape, like Mamie Eisenhower's finger-waved bangs. My sides were short and blunt and resembled one of the iconic Campbell Soup kids with the puffy, pink cheeks. The end result was that the haircut made my face as round and conspicuous as a full moon. It was everything that I *didn't* want.

Oblivious to my startled reaction, Mr. Murray said, "Well, I made you look gorgeous, didn't I?" Because I didn't want to get into any sort of confrontation with a "master stylist," I thanked him and smiled back without letting him know how disappointed I was.

After handing over my hard-earned money to the stone-faced, listless assistant at the front desk, I went immediately to the first-floor restroom to take a closer look at the "new" me. I was hoping that I had just been taken by surprise in the salon or hadn't had a good look at myself. Sadly, what I saw in the salon was how I actually looked. There was no way to rescue the cut. The bangs that I had been growing for months were now gone, exposing the large forehead that I had always hated. I wanted to elongate my face and not accentuate its roundness. Now, all I could think about were those silly Campbell Soup cans!

Over and over again, I tried to convince myself that the haircut really wasn't that bad. After all, if Mr. Murray was the hair expert, then he should know what looks best on me and I was probably wrong to feel that he had done a poor job. He, of all people, should be able to choose the best looks for his clients, right?

Still, I couldn't help but feel a pang of uncontrollable anguish and mouthed the words to no one in particular, "I hate my hair! I hate myself! I am so ugly! I will never be accepted in America!"

CHAPTER 2:

FEELING LOST

Graduating from Garfield High School in Seattle should have been an exciting time, but why didn't I feel that way? Perhaps it was because there were still so many questions looming before me about what I was going to do after graduation. Those concerns led to a lot of self-reflection and a much more subdued reaction to what is typically a happy and exciting milestone for most students.

After spending seven years attending American schools, I still wasn't comfortable with my English skills. It was difficult to imagine that I could catch up with my peers when I didn't understand classic American books like *The Adventures of Tom Sawyer*, which were required reading in school. The American culture was so foreign to me, which made it hard for me to understand, let alone relate to, many of the books that I was forced to read. I missed reading my old Japanese books that were mostly filled with tear-jerking dramas, depicting everyday life and the ever-present personal tragedies associated with it.

However, what really kept me from immersing myself in my studies were the countless hours I spent worrying about my Mother's failing health. The beautiful and vibrant woman that I once knew was now confined to a bed at the Firland Sanitarium in North Seattle; patients who resided there were plagued with an infectious, bacterial disease called tuberculosis (TB). Being the only child of a single, Nikkei[1] woman, I was completely dedicated to my Mother. The anguish that I felt seeing her suffer was so palpable that it was as if I was also suffering from the same disease.

One day, as I sat next to her bed, she held my hand and said, "Keiko, I'm so sorry that I've failed you. I caught TB in Japan during the war. Remember all of those boils we had on our bodies? My body was very weak because of the lack of food. I sacrificed my eating in order to keep you and Ojiichan[2] alive."

"I remember those days. I wanted you to buy three eggs... one for you, Ojiichan, and me... but you would only let me pick up two. I'm sorry I cried and screamed while yelling at you that you were mean not to let me buy the things I wanted to eat."

"Don't feel bad. You were so young and didn't understand why we were living under such harsh conditions. The good news is that we both lived and we also survived the bombings," Mother replied.

"I remember the American planes that circled over Kokura and the relentless dropping of their bombs," I said, remembering those frightening times during World War II.

"Keiko, remember one thing. Your life was spared at the last minute when the atomic bomb was dropped on Nagasaki, instead of Kokura. See your life as a gift and share this gift with others who need a helping hand. I believe there was a reason why you were allowed to survive and I know you know that, too."

---

1 Nikkei - a person or persons of Japanese descent, and their descendants, who emigrated from Japan.
2 Ojiichan - Grandfather

WATCH MY VIDEO:

Chapter 2: Feeling Lost

http://keikokayhirai.com/chapter-2-feeling-lost/

"Mother, one of the things I will always remember is how tired you looked after the War..."

"Yes. I knew I had contracted TB in Japan but I didn't want to tell you and I didn't want to worry you. You had enough of your own problems trying to adapt to life in this country. My being in and out of the hospital for the last six years has been tough on you. You've had no one to rely on since we arrived," she said, in an apologetic voice.

"Don't worry about me, Mother. I just want you to get well," I said, trying to show a confident, happy face even though I felt like crying.

"You were so happy with your school life in Japan, studying hard, knowing that you had to pass your exams to go to college. I felt terrible for lying to you and letting you believe we were coming to America for only a two-month visit with your Grandmother. It wasn't fair to you, but you were eleven years old and you would have lost your American citizenship if I didn't bring you to America that summer." She continued, "We came with only two suitcases in our hands and only had enough money to last for two months."

"And, you had to leave all of the inheritance that Ojiichan left for you in Japan," I reminded her.

"Now that you are about to graduate from high school, what do you think is next for you? Being the exceptional student you were in Japan, I hope you will continue your education here and attend the university," she said.

"Mother, I don't feel like I have the English skills I need to attend the university. But, don't worry about me. I will figure out something else I can do," I said, in an upbeat voice, so Mother would not notice how nervous and uncertain I was.

I felt alone, with no support, but it was important for me not to disappoint Mother. Deep down, I knew that I had to do something right away to start earning some income so that we could continue to survive.

Luckily, my cousin, Lilly, and my good friend, Saki, invited me to come along on a job interview at the Farwest Garment Factory, a local company that manufactured ski jackets. I quickly agreed to go with them.

When we arrived at Farwest's business office, we were told they had a large order of ski jackets that had to be shipped for the upcoming fall and winter ski season. After a brief interview, all three of us were hired and told to report to work the next morning.

On my first day of work, a supervisor led me to a small corner of the factory. There were shipping boxes everywhere, stacked right up to the ceiling. She said, "Your job is to fold these knitted cuffs for the sleeves of the jackets. You will have to work fast because these will go on the assembly line and then be forwarded to a waiting sewing crew. Do you understand?" she said.

"Yes, Ma'am," I answered.

I was determined to do my best on this job and went to work immediately. Even though I was shocked to see so many boxes of knitted cuffs in one place, I folded and folded and then folded some more. Once I finished with the first set of 100 cuffs, I arranged them neatly in a cardboard box and labeled them "Done." After that, I went back to folding the next 100 cuffs, and so on. I soon became so bored that I had a difficult time keeping my eyes open.

At the end of the third day, the supervisor came by and said,

"Kay, I've been watching your output for the last few days and it is extremely low. Obviously, this is not the right job for you. I think it would be best if you left this job."

Embarrassed, I slowly nodded my head. Without saying a word, I gathered my things and quietly left the factory.

This experience was especially demeaning for me because Lilly and Saki remained employed and both of them were eventually promoted to positions of greater responsibility.

After my humbling experience at Farwest, I was hired as an office helper at several different downtown offices. However, none of the jobs were very satisfying to me, so they all eventually ended the same way... in my termination.

What was I going to do? My Mother and I needed the money, but every job that I took felt so meaningless. The motivation to excel was what every manager wanted to see from their employees, but it was difficult for me to show any enthusiasm when I wasn't interested in the work that I was hired to do.

That fall, most of the girls I knew left their summer jobs to start their studies at the local university. Many of them wanted to become teachers. Others wanted to become nurses or accountants. I began to panic. What should I do? Where am I going in life? What kind of work would be meaningful to me?

In desperation, I went to the nearby library one afternoon to see if I could find a book that listed various career options. I thought that maybe there were some new careers that would interest me. After trudging up the steps to the double-entry doorway of the large building, I hesitantly entered. To my surprise, I saw an acquaintance named Janet, standing in the aisle between a set of book shelves. She had been a popular girl in high school and graduated a few years ahead of me. Hoping that she hadn't seen me, I quickly turned around and walked toward another aisle. In many ways, I was very awkward in social situations when I had to make small talk with popular classmates, especially those who were older than me. I tried hard not to get involved in lengthy conversations with any of them.

"Hi Kay!" Janet called out.

"Uh, oh. It's too late. She's already seen me," I thought to myself.

"Hi Janet," I replied, meekly.

Janet walked toward me and asked, "How are you? You graduated this year, right?"

"Yes, I did," I said.

"So, what are your plans now that you're out of school?" she asked.

"I don't know what I'm going to do and so I came here to see if there were any books that might steer me in the right direction," I replied, meekly.

"I know what you're going through because I was the same way after I graduated two years ago," she said.

"You were?" I asked, incredulously.

It was difficult for me to believe that a girl as popular and outgoing as Janet would have such a problem.

"I finally found my way and I love living my life now. When I get up every morning, I am excited to go to work," she said, enthusiastically.

"What do you do?" I asked.

"I went to a year's training in cosmetology and now I'm working at an upscale hair salon on Capitol Hill," she replied.

"You cut, color, and style people's hair?" I asked.

"Yes, I love the imaginative side of creating hair designs for people and I especially like the feeling that comes from being appreciated by my clients," she responded.

"Isn't it difficult to cut and style hair on people that you don't even know?" I asked apprehensively.

"I don't find that to be a problem because I view each client as a personal challenge to make them look nicer than when they entered the salon. If this sounds interesting, you should think about enrolling in a cosmetology school. I think you will find out pretty quickly whether you are suited for this type of work. There is an excellent school located in downtown Seattle, which is where I went," she said.

"Do you think I could be successful as a hair stylist, even though people might have a difficult time understanding me?" I asked.

"Kay, don't be so hard on yourself. You have a little accent, but I can understand you just fine. Besides, I remember in school that you were quite artistic. I think you would be very good at it," Janet said, encouragingly.

After thanking Janet, I joyfully left the library, forgetting all about the books I had intended to check out.

When I got home, I called Mother at the hospital and told her about my conversation with Janet. Even though I had already made up my mind that I was going to enroll at the cosmetology school, I wanted her blessing so that I could move forward with my idea. Thankfully, Mother was very happy with my decision.

I was thankful that Janet was so nice and helpful and not intimidating during our conversation that afternoon at the library. Any apprehensions that I had about starting a new career disappeared when she said, "Kay, let me know if you need help or if I can answer any questions for you. Just remember, I'm only a phone call away."

CHAPTER 3:

HOW I GOT MY START

For me, entering cosmetology school was like venturing into a new, strange world of fashion and beauty. The students were not at all like the girls I used to see in high school, who typically wore pastel-colored sweaters with white, rounded, cotton collars framing their necks. Good or bad, the cosmetology students were much more eclectic in their dress and mannerisms. The courses were dramatically different, as well. Although I was good at translating my ideas and thoughts onto paper using paints or pencils in regular schools, creating colors and shapes on human heads at this school was completely foreign to me.

At first, I didn't know how to talk to this diverse group of students who had arrived from all different parts of the country. I remember one young man, named Francoise, who had his hair dyed jet black. He told me that he was studying ballet in school, but was learning hair styling as a side business because he didn't want to starve while he was attempting to climb the ladder to fame in ballet dancing.

As far as instructors at the school, Ms. Joy was definitely my favorite. Her thick hair was cut short and colored with a maroon-hued, hair dye. She gave us firm directions and expected us to quickly learn the hair styling technique of finger waving and pin curling. "Students, I don't want to see sloppy partings and wimpy pin curls. I want to see the hair perfectly smooth and wrapped tightly around your fingers. Watch how I'm doing it," she warned, while demonstrating a flawless pin curl.

For the most part, I got along well with many of the teachers and students and even became good friends with a few of them. Beoma, a student from Alaska, became my best friend. We felt comfortable with each other because we were the only two in the school who didn't display outlandish colors or styles when it came to our hair and clothes. For several hours each day, we went through the normal routine of practicing with plastic mannequin heads and giving each other haircuts, styles, colors, and perms.

I graduated from the program in one year and started exploring the salons that dotted Seattle's downtown streets. With my license in hand and a list of potential salons that were recommended by Ms. Joy, I was bursting with enthusiasm and excited to begin my new journey. One of the things I will always remember is what she told me on the last day of class. She said, "Kay, don't let anyone tell you that you are not good enough. Tell them that you were trained by the best in the industry." With that great piece of advice, I was off to find my dream job.

As I went from salon to salon for interviews, my excitement was short-lived. Each interview ended abruptly when the salon owner or manager realized that I was a new cosmetology school graduate.

Time after time, I was told, "I'm sorry, but right now we are only hiring experienced stylists who can bring a large client base to our salon."

"I know I can build a good client list if you'd only give me a chance," I pleaded.

"Sorry, but try coming back when you've built your own clientele and we will consider hiring you," they responded.

My many pleas were to no avail. The series of negative responses was a crushing blow to my ego.

Dejected, but determined to visit every salon on my list, I made an appointment at the last one; it was located on the third floor of a downtown office building. With large, glass doors and a prominent black logo that read "Mr. Pesola," it was an impressive place – classy and credible, without the garish appearance of most of the salons I had previously visited.

I meekly walked into the salon after pushing open the heavy door. "Hello, my name is Kay and I'm here for my 2:00 p.m. appointment with Mr. Pesola," I said. I tried to project some semblance of confidence, but it was difficult given how other salons had written me off. The receptionist smiled at me and said, "Oh sure. He will be out as soon as he finishes up with his 1:00 p.m. client."

I was escorted to a corner of the reception room. After waiting about thirty minutes and getting increasingly nervous, Mr. Pesola finally arrived and greeted me with a handshake and a smile.

"I understand that you are a new cosmetology graduate and are looking for a job as a stylist," he said. At least he hadn't kicked me out yet, I mumbled to myself.

"Yes," I answered hopefully, "I was wondering if you had a job opening here. I really like how your salon looks."

I was expecting the same type of rejection that I had received from everyone else and couldn't believe what I was hearing when he said, "Yes, you came at the right time. We have the perfect job for you."

"You do?" I replied, wanting to jump up and down with excitement.

"Olga, our salon assistant, recently went to visit her family in Sweden for the summer. You can fill in at her position for the next three months."

"So, I'm not being hired as a stylist?"

"Eventually you will be, but, for now, you will be taking over in her assistant position," he replied.

"What does Olga do?" I asked nervously, worried about what I was about to hear.

"Olga does a lot of things, but we'll start you off slowly. Your main job will be to clean and sanitize the hair brushes, do the laundry, sweep hair off the floors, and run out to pick up our lunches when asked," he responded.

I couldn't keep myself from showing a certain amount of disappointment. Sensing it, Mr. Pesola immediately flashed me a big grin and said, "Don't worry. I know you want to work as a stylist. This is only the beginning! You'll have plenty of time to acclimate yourself to this industry and one day you will be an accomplished hair stylist!"

"May I ask about my pay?" I said, changing the subject.

"I pay my stylists the same as other salons in the industry – a 40% commission for every client you serve. You, however, will receive a set stipend for the work I just described. When Olga returns, I will put you out on the floor so that you can work on commission."

"You'll help me get paying clients into my chair?" I asked.

"No," he said firmly, quickly erasing that notion. "That is up to you. Every client that comes through our front door belongs to someone who works here and everyone is working to increase their commissions. So, be careful. Anyone who steals another stylist's clients is automatically banned from my salon."

I couldn't help but be intimidated by his response.

"So, how should I go about finding clients?" I asked.

"It is up to you to decide how badly you want to succeed. You have to get yourself out there and market yourself! Get some business cards printed and hand them out everywhere you go. Even people you pass on the street are potential customers!" he emphasized.

I instantly hated his idea because I just wanted to be a hair stylist – not a saleswoman! On the other hand, I thought, I am lucky just to receive a job offer within the industry. Even though it isn't my preferred position as a stylist, it is at least a start. Besides, I couldn't stand the thought of visiting another salon and being turned down again.

After a few seconds of thinking it over, there was only one thing to say… "Thank you, Mr. Pesola, I accept your offer," I responded, enthusiastically.

"Good. I expect to see you here at 9:00 a.m. tomorrow morning," he replied.

It was a busy salon with six stylists. The job description that Mr. Pesola had outlined during my job interview was accurate. I cleaned, sanitized, and dried buckets of brushes and combs all day. In between, I swept hair clippings from under each of the styling chairs, cleaned off the counter tops, served tea to clients, and ran around to various nearby restaurants to pick up lunches for the stylists.

The glamour of working in a hair salon quickly wore off, however, and I didn't feel much different from the time I spent folding cuffs at the Farwest Garment Factory. "Is this it?" I began to wonder, "Will I get any further? Will I ever get to style the hair of my own customers?"

A few more weeks rolled by. It was another typical, boring day and I was in the back room picking hair off the soiled brushes piled up in a large, plastic bin. In the middle of my daydreams and internal frustrations, someone walked up and lightly tapped me on the shoulder. It was Jean, one of the salon's stylists, who had been working at the salon with her husband for about six months. Jean had bright, copper-colored hair that was styled so perfectly it was hard to believe it wasn't a wig. I admired her more than anyone else in the salon. She always made her clients look beautiful. To her credit, she acted in a more professional manner than the other stylists. Jean's demeanor was more like an instructor than a hair stylist. She was always pleasant, friendly, and had great customer service skills. Howard, Jean's husband, was also very kind, but more laid back, with a relaxed personality that didn't come across as arrogant like most of the other high-end hair stylists I had seen and met. Even though he was very competent, he didn't seem to have the same artistic talent for designing hair and looked more like a fifth-grade math teacher by the way he dressed.

"Kay," Jean began, "You probably don't know this, but Howard and I moved here from Chicago several months ago to see if we could make a go of things. We have grown to love Seattle and are ready to make our move permanent. As a result, we are going to give our notice at the salon next week, fly back to Chicago to sell our house, and then move back to Seattle to build a life here."

Surprised at the news, I was wide-eyed. "How soon will you be returning?"

"If everything goes well, we should be back in about three months. We'll be building a new salon of our own in the Nettleton Apartments, not far from downtown. We have already signed the lease!" she exclaimed.

I hesitated to make a comment, not wanting to read too much into what she was saying.

"I've been watching you," she continued. "I like your work ethic and I think you have great potential in this industry if only someone would take you under their wing and train you. I'd like to be that person. So, consider this a job offer with our new salon. When Howard and I get back from Chicago, I will call you. At that time, if you are still interested, please consider giving your notice to leave the salon."

She then looked at me intently and started nodding. As she was doing this, her face broke out in a big smile, as if she wanted me to agree with her.

It felt like a dream. I thought, "Surely this sort of thing doesn't happen to people like me, does it?"

Jean glanced at me again, raised her eyebrows, and smiled. "Well?" she asked.

"Yes, yes!" I cried.

CHAPTER 4:

MY INVALUABLE TRAINING

"Trend Coiffures" was located in the lobby of the Nettleton Apartments in downtown Seattle. On my first day of work, it was almost ready to open its doors to the public. Before that happened, though, a lot of work had to be done. When I arrived early that morning, I immediately started lining the salon's shelves and organizing the hair color products and permanent wave lotions. Afterwards, I wiped down the dusty mirrors and styling chairs that had just been unloaded from the delivery truck. During all of this activity, I couldn't help but feel that this was the beginning of something important and special in my life. I was finally going to find out what it was like to work in a "real" salon. I was so happy that I wanted to dance across the salon floor and skip through the bright sunlight that was streaming in through the large, floor-length windows. This feeling was exactly what I had dreamed about when I first entered cosmetology school.

After the salon was open for a few weeks, Jean often asked me to take care of the salon when she was gone. I was proud that she entrusted me with so much responsibility. To learn more about running the business end of a salon, I paid attention to the types of meetings she went to and I always asked her questions about how she managed to keep things running so smoothly.

After observing her day-to-day activities for a while, I noticed that Jean was a terrific marketer. She often attended gatherings at the Women's University Club and the Seattle Chamber of Commerce to network with her peers. She also knocked on the doors of high-end women's boutiques to introduce herself and promote her new, upscale salon. I guessed that she must have handed out business cards by the hundreds. With her winning personality and professional image, she definitely gave everyone the confidence that she knew what she was doing.

"Kay, today I have an important job for you," she said to me one day. "Take this stack of fliers and leave one of them at the front door of every apartment unit in this building. If you see people in the hallways, smile and introduce yourself. Promote our salon by telling them about the beautiful hairdos we can style for them." And so, I rode the elevator to each floor and left dozens of "Welcome Packets" that included a 20% off discount coupon. Many of the building's 350 residents appreciated the invitation and made an appointment with us.

With Jean's help, I eventually got the opportunity to cut hair and slowly developed my own client list. Rowland and David, however, were the two most popular stylists and were always booked. They were chatty and flirty and had no trouble flattering the female clients who believed every compliment they threw their way.

"Oh, Rowland, I love the style you gave me today! I know I'll get rave reviews at the party I'm attending tonight!" Mrs. Johnson exclaimed.

"Of course you will! You look downright gorgeous and no

doubt will be the envy of all the women at the party!" he responded, enthusiastically.

A little confused, I continued watching from the other end of the design floor. Why did Mrs. Johnson think that she looked so good? In my opinion, her haircut was severe and flat and didn't do anything to soften her angular features.

One evening, after everyone else had left the salon, I gathered up the nerve to approach Jean and asked her, "Why do women admire Rowland's and David's work so much? The only time women book an appointment with me is when one of them goes on vacation. Even when they sit in my chair, they refuse to let me think on my own. They just ask me to duplicate whatever Rowland or David has done for them!" I was frustrated and it showed, but I was glad that I could finally get that off of my chest.

Of course, Jean knew exactly what I was talking about.

"Kay," she said, "the residents who live at the Nettleton Apartments are doctors, lawyers, and other professionals. Most of our clients are their wives. Remember, they could potentially become your best customers, too, because you certainly have the skills; what you lack, however, is the "stage presence" that Rowland and David possess. You simply don't project enough confidence in yourself. Unless you learn to do that, no one will believe that you're good at styling hair."

"First of all, you must dress and act in a way that is comparable to their lifestyles. For example, most of these women travel all over the world and shop at high-end boutiques that carry the latest designer clothes. They get haircuts, styles, and colors in Paris and Rome and they want a similar experience here in Seattle," she explained.

"But, what can I do?" I asked, not fully understanding what she was trying to tell me.

"For starters, you should avoid wearing your homemade, polyester dresses. I know it will be hard for you to spend good money on designer-brand clothes made of pure cotton and wool, but you should look at it as an investment in your career. And, in addition, you are painfully shy. You don't seem to know how to be at ease with your clients. Let me work with you to polish up your speaking skills so that you can be more comfortable," she offered.

I listened intently to Jean's advice. The next opportunity I had, I went shopping at the Frederick and Nelson department store to invest in a few designer clothes with labels like Calvin Klein and Ralph Lauren. I also purchased a pair of high-heeled, slip-on shoes.

"Oh, you look great!" Jean exclaimed when I showed up for work the next morning, wearing my new clothes. Upon hearing that comment, I instantly felt a lot better about all of the money I had spent. "I just know this will give you more confidence when you are working with our clients. Now, you look just as credible as Rowland and David," she said, with a smile on her face.

That was just the beginning of my hands-on training. As I soon discovered, there was never a dull moment working for Jean. If my work wasn't up to her standards or I couldn't please a customer, she kept me at the salon after closing time to drill me on techniques to improve my cutting, coloring, and styling skills. I was very grateful for her strict attention to detail and the fact that she was willing to take so much of her personal time to make sure that I did things correctly. We often stayed at the salon until 10:00 p.m. at night to practice on mannequins and style up-dos with firm back-combing. When I was done, my hair styles were so perfectly executed that they would stay intact for a week!

I appreciated and valued Jean's personal attention and knew that her careful guidance would eventually help me to become a successful and sought-after hair stylist. I often felt that Jean saw me as the daughter she never had and was willing to help because she liked my obedient nature and desire to learn the trade.

At the end of my second year at the salon, I was still up to my elbows learning the trade and the fundamentals of running a business. During one particularly busy afternoon, Jean called me into her office as I was finishing the last bite of a sandwich during my lunch break. I knew it must have been something serious and I was right.

"Kay, I hate to break bad news to you like this, but I've been diagnosed with an extremely fast-growing type of cancer. My doctor told me that I have to quit working while I receive my treatments. I argued with him about this course of action, but he explained that chemicals will be injected into my body and have debilitating effects," she said, managing a weak smile.

She went on to elaborate that her health had not been good for some time and that, as a result, she and Howard had made the difficult decision to sell the salon. I was shocked because I certainly wasn't expecting *that* kind of news. It was like a rug had suddenly been pulled out from under me.

"Oh, no! I am so sorry to hear that," I said, gathering myself. "Is there anything I can do to help?"

"Don't worry. The two young men who are planning to buy this salon are smart guys. They both graduated from Seattle University with business degrees and should be able to quickly grow this business a lot quicker than I have been able to do during the last few years."

"But, they're not hair stylists, are they? How will they know how to run the salon?" I inquired.

"You're right, they are not stylists. But, business is business. It's probably better that they aren't stylists. I told them that I've groomed you and that you will be able to help them a great deal in running the salon," she said encouragingly.

"Really?" I asked, not entirely convinced at the time.

"Yes, of course. They are counting on you to help them with ordering our products and continuing to offer the highest level of customer service," she said.

Two weeks later, Jean and Howard were abruptly gone and I found myself working for two young businessmen who dressed in suits and ties.

The first thing they did after taking over was to hire a receptionist for the front desk and one additional stylist. Because of her unprofessional demeanor, I did not have a good feeling about the new receptionist. I was also annoyed because I was not used to having anyone call me "Honey." The appearance of the new stylist was also a bit alarming. She was dressed so casually, wearing tight, frayed jeans and a t-shirt with rhinestone trim around the neckline. Jean had always demanded that we dress in a simple and tasteful manner and these two new employees demonstrated anything but that. For me, it was difficult to watch all of these dramatic changes take place; the salon felt and looked so different.

After three months, I could not look past the changes. The salon's front doors would often be closed when I arrived at work in the morning because no one had shown up on time to open them. Once, I had to wait outside the salon for thirty minutes with my first client of the day standing anxiously by my side. I was extremely embarrassed and apologized profusely for this unacceptable business practice. Although I tried to remain optimistic, the downward slide continued.

My patience finally ran out when one of my paychecks failed to clear the bank. When I asked the owners about the "insufficient funds" stamp on the check, they told me not to worry because there had been a mix-up at the bank. With a straight face, they promised that there would be sufficient funds to cover my bounced check by the following week.

Three returned paychecks later, I knew that the salon was in financial trouble. Now, there was only one thing to do. I gave my notice and walked away from my first real job in the salon industry – a place that I initially loved so much and would never forget.

CHAPTER 5:

BACK ON THE STREET

I was back on the street again looking for work. It was disappointing, but I felt more confident this time because I had acquired many new skills and much needed experience while working at Jean's hair salon. But, I should have anticipated that there would be more bumps in the road.

Over and over again, I was rudely awakened to the reality of the industry as I failed to correctly answer the question potential employers always asked me: "How many clients can you bring to my salon if I hire you?"

Thinking that things might be different outside of downtown Seattle, I decided to apply at a high-end salon called "Emery's," which was located on the edge of the city. The owner/stylist, Mr. Emery, opened his salon after building his reputation behind a chair at Frederick and Nelson's department store in Seattle. Frederick and Nelson was widely known as a place where many well-to-do women shopped and had their hair styled.

When I arrived at the salon, I was greeted by an older reception-ist who looked like she had just stepped out of a high-end boutique. Her silver hair was styled into a smooth, page-boy cut and her white blouse and black skirt were simply striking. A beautiful flower ar-rangement of roses and baby's breath sat on a corner table. I stared at the tastefully designed arrangement while sitting in an antique chair covered in beige brocade, waiting for Mr. Emery to arrive. In this well-staged and formal setting, I felt completely out of my element.

Out of nowhere, a familiar face and voice appeared from around the corner. It was Francoise! I had studied with him at cosmetology school and instantly recalled that he was somewhat flamboyant and extremely creative when it came to styling hair for the school's cus-tomers.

"Thank you for visiting our salon today, Mrs. Wagner. I en-joyed serving you and am happy that your hair came out so stunning-ly," I heard him say to his client. He noticed me as he abruptly pivot-ed back and faced the hallway.

"Kay, is that really you? It's been years! Are you applying for a job here?" he asked.

"Yes, but I didn't know that you worked here," I said, apologet-ically.

"Mr. Emery is a very nice man. I will put in a good word for you. It would be fun for us to work together. Just like old times!" he exclaimed.

Francoise gave me a glowing review and introduction just as Mr. Emery walked in to find us talking. "Kay and I attended the same cosmetology school and we graduated together in 1961," he said. "I hope you'll hire her. She is a very nice person and was very good in school." I appreciated the quick wink of his eye, as Francoise walked back into the hallway.

I could see that Mr. Emery's demeanor changed after Fran-coise's recommendation. At that moment, I thought I might actually have a shot at the job.

"Kay, Francoise is one of my top stylists, but I don't know anything about you. What have you been doing since you graduated from school?" he asked, as he began the interview.

"I have been working at Trend Coiffures for the last three years," I responded.

"Oh, yes, Jean's salon, he said. "She really knows how to network and has done a wonderful job of building her salon. Can I ask you why you decided to leave?"

"Jean was unfortunately diagnosed with cancer and was forced to sell her salon. The new owners are struggling and they couldn't maintain the systems that Jean had put into place. But, I was lucky to work there for as long as I did. Jean trained me in all of the aspects of hair design. I believe I can please your customers with quality haircuts, colors, and foils," I explained.

"Do you have any clients that you can bring with you?" he inquired. Of course, he had to ask.

I responded sheepishly, "No, I don't."

"Really? he asked, incredulously. That's hard for me to believe. Well, why not?"

"I didn't think it was ethical for me to ask the clients that I had built up at Jean's salon to move with me to another salon. Those clients were brought in by Jean, who spent hours of her time recruiting them," I explained.

While taking a quick glance at his face, I got the impression that Mr. Emery thought I was out of my mind!

"Then, how do you expect to get a decent commission in a new salon?" he asked.

"I am willing to start fresh here," I said, with determination. "I know I won't be making much at the beginning because a 40% commission on nothing is still nothing. But, I'm confident that with my skills in hair design, I can build a good base of loyal clients again."

Fortunately, Mr. Emery understood my reasoning. I got the job and was eager to quickly get back on my feet

There was no training at Mr. Emery's salon. The senior stylists did not share their personal techniques and hid their color formulas so that no one else could copy them. Everyone kept to themselves and jealously guarded their clients. After only a few months on the job, I watched dozens of stylists come and go. They were given no support and most had to leave because they weren't able to make a living income. After working at a supportive place like Trend Coiffures, Mr. Emery's salon was a difficult environment to work in.

I quickly realized that I would have to take responsibility for my own education and improvement. After doing a little research, I enrolled in Vidal Sassoon's (a famous hair designer from England) training courses, paying what sometimes felt like an absurd amount of money to learn precision haircutting techniques straight from London. All of the haircuts we learned in class had a blunt, hard edge to them, but I practiced hour after hour to create a softer look that I thought would be more flattering to a woman's facial features. Every night, I looked through the latest magazines to train my eye to recognize the classic beauty and fashion styles that would endure.

Eventually, I developed my own style of hair design that resulted in a quieter, softer, and airier feel that flattered women of all ages. My haircuts were more durable, so that the styles held their shape longer than what clients were used to. By adopting my own style of cutting, I steadily gained a good reputation and grew my client base.

Even with the steep learning curve, my job at Mr. Emery's salon, with its model-like receptionists and defensive co-workers, gratefully took me through the next six years of my life. The life-changing events of getting married, having two children, the death of my beloved mother, and a traumatic car accident that left my young daughter with a brain injury, all took place among the countless days of guiding my clients through Mr. Emery's pristine hallways. One of the things that kept me going was my determination to perfect every technique that I could.

With time off to celebrate family joys and deal with family sorrows, I was constantly starting over to build my clientele. I took three months off after each childbirth, as well as after my daughter's traumatic accident. Each time, I came back to work, I found that other stylists had taken over my clients who I had worked so hard to get. I received small paychecks for weeks until I could build my client base again.

It wasn't hard for one stylist to steal a client away from another. I constantly overheard conversations between stylists and clients that went something like this:

Stylist: "Who cut your hair last?"

Client: "Why do you ask?"

Stylist: "This isn't a good haircut. She obviously didn't understand your hair. I can tell because she cut your right side shorter than your left."

Stylists stabbed each other in the back because of their greed and also to make themselves look better. It was a constant sales job to convince your clients that you were the only one who could possibly understand their hair and its peculiarities.

The best that a stylist could hope for in terms of increasing or improving their skills was to receive training from a senior stylist in exchange for helping to shampoo their clients. Any training that occurred typically took place after normal business hours when everyone was exhausted from working all day.

I realized that the industry I worked in was not like other careers. In the cosmetology industry, the stylist's value to a salon is measured by the number of regular clients that are tied to them, not by the stylist's level of skill. And, no matter how long a stylist works for a salon, the stylist has to re-build his or her clientele if he or she takes a leave of absence to deal with family matters. In this system, no clients means no pay. The only job security stylists have is the number of clients who will continue to seek them out after a leave of absence or a move to another salon.

After a few years, Emery's became an increasingly miserable place to work. Although I seriously tried to make the best of it, I was discouraged and confused. Why was the cosmetology industry so irrational? Why was it based solely on commission or chair rentals? Where is the teamwork that is needed to help stylists grow and learn from one another and work cooperatively with all of the salon's clients? How was a stylist supposed to learn new skills and progress if they were always being kicked back to the bottom of the career ladder by their own peers? I needed answers to these questions if I wanted to continue to work in the industry.

One evening, I approached Mr. Emery in his office as the salon was closing.

"Mr. Emery, I have been meaning to talk to you about my concerns when new stylists are hired," I began. "I noticed that many of them don't stay at the salon for very long. If they received some training while they are working, they might have a better chance to grow their careers here in your salon."

"Yes, go on," he replied.

"If everyone received training and stable paychecks, you could have a salon where each stylist would have the skills to serve any of the salon's customers and make them happy," I said, feeling more confident.

"Hmmm," he acknowledged, seemingly deep in thought.

"I think if you promoted a team concept where everyone helped each other instead of having stylists work solely for themselves, you could have a more supportive work environment where everyone could grow to their full potential. In addition, customers would ultimately have a better salon experience."

"So, this is what you wanted to talk to me about?" he asked.

"Yes, I've wanted to talk to you about this for a while because this back-stabbing type of work environment really bothers me," I replied.

"Well, Kay, I have wanted to talk to you as well. You just don't seem to be fitting in around here. Now, I know why. It is because you have your own ideas of how a salon should be run," he said.

"Please, Mr. Emery, I pleaded. "I know that your salon could be so much better." As soon as the words left my mouth, I knew I had lost the battle.

"Kay, don't try to tell me how I should run my business. If you have ideas, open your own salon instead of trying to change mine," he responded, his face growing increasingly red and angry-looking.

And so, I left. It was now clear to me that in order to make my vision of teamwork, qualified stylists, and happy clients a reality, I would have to open my own salon.

CHAPTER 6:

SHOW ME THE MONEY

After a restless night of endlessly rehearsing the answers to questions about the business plan for my new salon, I woke up at 6:00 a.m. the next morning, bleary-eyed and nervous. In a few hours, I was going to what I hoped would be a life-changing appointment with a banker in downtown Seattle.

I knew that I needed to present myself in a way that warranted the $40,000 loan that I was requesting to start my salon. A conservative, navy blue jacket and skirt seemed appropriate, along with a pair of black, high-heeled shoes. The scratchy wool of the jacket made my neck itch, but I hoped that my professional attire would make me look more like a businesswoman than a hair stylist. Besides, if I got the loan, all of this dressing up would be worth it. I certainly couldn't afford to come across as an ill-prepared entrepreneur who didn't know how to do anything without a pair of scissors or a curling iron in her hands.

To make certain that I wasn't going to be late, I arrived extra early at the bank. It was in a soaring, multiple-story building with large, glass double-doors and a spacious waiting area filled with expensive, but uncomfortable furniture. The ambiance was impressive, while at the same time, intimidating. After about five minutes, a man in a tailored black suit walked up to me and confidently shook my hand.

Greg, as he introduced himself, was the manager of the bank. He was friendly and had a nice smile. As we started to chat, however, his mannerisms displayed the height of arrogance that made me feel defensive and a bit taken aback. We continued to exchange pleasantries in his small, but immaculately clean office. The only sign that someone used the office was a small stack of file folders that lay neatly on one side of the mahogany desk.

"I'm here to see if you would give me a loan to start my new business, a hair salon," I said a little sheepishly.

"A hair salon? Not the sort of business we typically work with, but I am willing to listen. You need a sound business plan. You brought one, didn't you?" he said.

I tentatively pulled out my carefully-written, ten-page business plan and handed it to him.

If you'll excuse me, I'll step out for a moment to take a look at this, alright?" he said. He was gone before I finished nodding my head in agreement.

My mind raced as I sat alone in his office. Would my plan make sense to him? What was I doing sitting here? What if I can't explain my vision to him? I felt like I was stuck in that room for hours, the walls quickly closing in around me as if I were in a jail cell.

After several minutes, Greg returned in his pressed suit with his dark, thinning hair combed back neatly, almost as if it was pasted to his head. His leather shoes were polished to an impeccable shine. Suddenly, I wanted to run out of the room and forget about every dream I had ever had about owning my own salon.

He walked to his desk and slowly sat down in his leather chair.

"What makes you think you have the skills to run a business?" he asked, looking directly in my eyes.

"I know so much about the cosmetology industry," I said. "I've learned a lot from working for various salons and owners, but I know I can do a better job for my customers and stylists. I know how to ensure that my customers get a great haircut from every stylist I employ."

"What do you mean by that?"

"I don't know of any salon that provides consistent, quality service to their clients. Young stylists are hired right out of cosmetology school and are expected to build their own clientele without any training. They are paid a commission for every client they serve, but it is difficult for them to stay employed because of the commission structure that is used at most salons. A 50% commission on a few clients a day hardly amounts to a living wage."

"So, you have a plan to help more stylists succeed in their jobs?"

I straightened up and replied, "Yes, I do. The key is for every entry-level stylist to receive training in customer service as well as to continually improve their technical skills. Cosmetology schools don't do enough to ensure that their students' future customers will have a good, ongoing experience in a salon. And..."

"Kay, what kind of formal business training have you had?" he inquired, as he abruptly cut me off.

"I have been reading a lot of books on how to start a business as well as attending night classes at a local community college."

"Does your father own a business? Did you learn anything while growing up and working in a family business?"

"No one in my family has had a business. I was only four-months old when my father lost his life while serving in the Japanese Navy during World War II. My mother became ill shortly after she brought me to America."

"So then, English is not your first language. I was wondering where your accent came from. Do you have any post-secondary education?"

I stared at him, not knowing exactly what he was inquiring about.

"I'm asking if you have ever attended college," he responded.

"No. I have been taking care of my mother who has tuberculosis and I didn't have the confidence to go beyond high school. I was educated in Kokura, Japan through fifth-grade and was one of the top students in a very tough, educational system. But, all of that ended when my mother moved us to the United States. Because of the change in cultures, I was uncomfortable and ended up at the bottom of my class." Extremely nervous, I felt like I was rambling.

Greg quickly shifted the conversation. "I think you did a good job of creating your business plan," he said, thumbing through the pages. "I can see you've put a lot of care into it and that you thoroughly researched your competition in the cosmetology industry. But from where I'm standing, it's still not realistic. You want to go head-to-head with the traditional business practices of an entire industry and you didn't write anything about wanting to create a profitable business. In my world, that's the only thing that matters."

I was reeling from what he was saying and felt like I was on the receiving end of a bad lecture.

"You are asking the bank to lend you $40,000 of start-up money to add to the $20,000 you already have, but you haven't told me how you're going to pay the bank back."

Looking down at the floor, I whispered, "I know I can do this." I was humiliated and wanted to disappear into a hole, never to return.

"Do you understand the importance of cash?" he demanded. "You won't have any unless you're aggressive and that's what's missing from your business plan. Listen, Kay. We are a bank. The bottom line is that we need to know that you can pay back the money you want to borrow from us. It is the only way that we can stay in business."

He slipped my business plan back into its folder and pushed it toward me.

"I am sorry, but we won't be able to work with you on this. I suggest you go to another bank that has a department that helps minority women like yourself to start their own business. A bank like that may be willing to take a look at your plan and qualify you for a loan."

Numb from our discussion, I thanked him and left the bank. The busy Seattle streets glistened in the sunlight. They were filled with people who were completely unaware that my hopes and dreams had just been broken into a million pieces.

Two months passed. I re-worked my business plan and focused more attention on how I would manage my cash flow and reach profitability. I submitted my revised plan to three banks, including one that had promoted itself as having a department that handled minority women-owned businesses. Each one sent me a cold, but polite letter of rejection. A harsh reality started to sink in.

When I was at one my lowest points, I received a phone call from James, a CPA who was married to a good friend of mine. He told me to call the SBA office located in downtown Seattle.

"Call the what?" I asked, "I have never heard of them."

"The Small Business Administration is a federal government agency; its mission is to encourage more entrepreneurship in the United States. They offer different kinds of support to people who want to become business owners," James said.

"Why would they want to do that?"

"Because 70% of the workers in our country are employed by small businesses. The government is interested in helping people start local shops and factories," he replied.

This information amazed me. I had never seen myself as part of a bigger picture, as someone who might help our country towards economic prosperity by starting my own business.

My visit to the SBA office on the eighth floor of a skyscraper in downtown Seattle was reassuring. I felt comfortable, like I belonged there. The SBA's loan officer listened to my presentation and looked through my business plan. He read my vision and mission statement out loud, "To be a revolutionary business that improves the lives of the people we serve... Innovation, Quality, and Value...We will strive to exceed our customers' expectations."

I sat there in silence, waiting for him to say, "Where's your cash?"

Instead, he said, "Your proposal is quite refreshing. I like it."

My initial excitement was soon suppressed by the thick packet of paper that I was handed a minute later.

"I know this is a lot of paperwork, the loan officer said, "but this level of detailed information is necessary. If your loan is approved, we'll be working with a partner bank. The SBA will be the guarantor of your loan, so if you don't succeed in your business, the partner bank will still get its money back."

Completing the 60-page application took two months of grueling, detailed, and tedious work. In the end, however, going through this process taught me how to develop a thorough and comprehensive business plan. A few weeks later, I held my head up high and felt justifiably proud when I turned my completed paperwork into the SBA office.

Five weeks later, I received a letter from the SBA. It read, in part:

"Dear Kay Hirai. We are happy to inform you that your loan request #759810 has been approved by the Small Business Administration of America. Please contact us at 206-284-0904 so we may assist you in the next steps of your loan process."

"Yes! Yes! Yes!" I shouted at the top of my lungs. I was determined not to disappoint the SBA and the faith they had just entrusted in me. Not only would I succeed in my business, but I was also determined to pay back *every penny* of the SBA loan. Deep down, I also wanted to show all of the banks that turned me down that they had made a mistake in not investing in me. I certainly believed I could make my plan work, even if they didn't.

CHAPTER 7:

HOW COME I'M NOT HAPPY?

I opened my first salon in a new shopping mall located on Broadway Avenue, a busy street in Seattle's vibrant Capitol Hill business district. I named the salon "Hair on Broadway," a catchy name that I thought was appropriate for the area. Located on the second floor of the Broadway Arcade mall, my salon was fairly spacious with a modern décor. During the design phase, a local architect offered me some guidance. He told me, "Don't go with the status quo; make your salon "pop" so that you stand out from the crowd." I followed his advice and one of the first things I did was purchase a set of red sofas to catch the attention of passersby, as well as people who entered the front door of my salon.

The salon had a big front window with a black-and-chrome Hair on Broadway sign hanging in the middle of it. Unlike most reception desks, I selected a white Formica counter that curved around in the shape of a half-circle. For the convenience of our customers, I placed a small calendar and a sleek pen container with elegant pens on the counter. These items would allow clients to conveniently schedule their next appointments before they left the salon. My goal was to keep everything in the salon immaculately clean and simple. Walking into the design area of the salon, clients would see a wide, open space with mirrors on both sides. Black leather chairs sat in front of each mirror. The dark hardwood floor gave the room a feeling of stability and character.

The adjoining businesses in the enclosed mall were a collection of quirky boutiques, a high-end flower shop, a small gift store, and a European fabric store that carried the well-known Marimekko fabrics. I enjoyed shopping in all the stores, but my favorite was the coffee shop; the barista knew me by name and brewed my favorite coffee drink when I walked in the door. Every morning I stopped in before opening the salon and my barista asked me, "How are your kids? How is your business doing?" Even though we were from seemingly different worlds, I enjoyed talking with her, thinking nothing of the ring in her nose and the rose tattoo on her arm.

In the third year of business, I invited my good friend, Marie, to become a business partner. We had worked in a previous salon together, I trusted her judgment, and I enjoyed working with her. Similar to my daughter, Sheri, Marie's younger sister had also been hit by a car and sustained a traumatic brain injury. Our experiences of helping loved ones with brain injuries gave us a common bond. After Marie became my business partner, running the salon didn't seem as lonely as when I was doing it on my own. Almost unheard of in a fledgling business, Marie and I were able to draw a decent salary from the very beginning. After eight years of hard work, everything looked like it was going well. Our families and friends deemed the business venture a big success.

In reality, however, it was a different story. Most nights, I tossed and turned, waking up every few hours with a gnawing feeling in my stomach. I had run a successful business and overcome a hundred obstacles, figuratively thumbing my nose at naysayers along the way. Instead of feeling triumphant, though, I felt like a hamster running on a wheel.

One sunny day, after another sleepless night, I gritted my teeth and went to a nearby park to seriously think about what was bothering me. I wanted to face the frustrations and issues that I had been avoiding in the hope that they would simply fade away. After a lot of soul searching, I realized one of my main frustrations was that the people I hired to work in my salon were not really *my* employees. They essentially rented a chair from the salon, worked on commission, and were their own bosses. Many of them joined the salon because of the relatively high-commission. What usually happened, however, was that they left the salon after working only a few months. They had no interest in learning new skills. With the constant turnover, I was unable to establish and sustain the high standard of customer service that was so important to me. It was painful to watch my customers walk out of the salon with mediocre color jobs and unflattering haircuts. Sadly, my "temporary" stylists also often treated customers in a condescending or disinterested manner. This revolving-door of stylists was certainly not helping my business, employees, or the customers. I was hoping for better days ahead, but the chances of reaching that goal were looking pretty dim.

As I continued my "soul searching," I realized that I had very little in common with the colleagues I met when I attended industry workshops. Many were self-absorbed and arrogant - even pretentious. We worked in luxurious salons and focused so much on hair and beauty that we tended to forget who we really were or what was taking place in the outside world. I couldn't stop thinking about all of the people who needed our help but couldn't afford our services. A well-designed, flattering hair style made a powerful statement. Executed by a professional stylist and accompanied by a few kind words, could immediately enhance a person's self-esteem. I often witnessed these dramatic changes right in front of my own eyes. Watching clients being completely transformed by their experiences in the salon was fun to watch. They would come into the salon with their heads down, their shoulders stooped, and their eyes looking off to the side, but leave with their heads held high, a self-assured smile, and an extra bounce in their step.

Deep down, I realized that I wanted something different from what most of my colleagues were looking for. It was probably because I always remembered my Mother's wise counsel, "Keiko, you are a lucky girl. You escaped the atomic bomb during World War II in Japan. The city of Kokura, where we lived, was spared the devastating effects of the bomb. Your life is a gift; don't ever forget that. You have many talents. Use them to help others as you live your life."

As I thought about what I wanted for my salon, I always remembered my Mother's motivating words. I realized that one of my biggest priorities was to create a salon that welcomed a wider community of people and supported those who needed a helping hand. There were hundreds of people all around me who would never have the opportunity to visit a salon like Hair on Broadway. I needed to do something for them even if they couldn't pay. Giving back was an intrinsic part of my life's circle of harmony. Certainly, salon owners could contribute to the local community and do more than simply take money from their clients, couldn't they? From what I could tell, it seemed as if no one thought it was a business' responsibility to extend a helping hand to those in need. Why did this kind of thinking exist? The reason soon became apparent to me... philanthropy is the opposite of creating a profit.

After this moment of self-discovery, my unhappiness and sleepless nights eventually disappeared. I wanted to be successful, but more importantly, I wanted to do good things. After making appointments with my CPA and my attorney, I explained to both of them what I wanted to focus on in my business. In nice terms, they told me that I was in the wrong line of work if philanthropy was my ultimate goal. "Good business owners are only focused on one thing and that's profit," my CPA said. "You, on the other hand, are more concerned about the well-being of your employees and the community. It's a nice sentiment, but a major concern for me is that I am not sure that you will be able to sustain that business model for very long." My attorney echoed those same thoughts, almost word for word. I walked out of both of their offices wondering if I should even be in business.

As I reflected on those discussions, I realized that I had faced worse obstacles and challenges in my life and had survived. Although it was an extremely tough decision, I made up my mind to dissolve my business partnership with Marie. Doing that would give me the freedom I needed to build a life around my priorities. To that end, I developed a list of "wants." I wanted to find the passion and drive to be a community-focused business leader. I wanted my customers to receive the best possible service, haircuts, and colors. I wanted happy and thoughtful employees who wanted to learn new skills, and I wanted to attract clients who agreed with my philanthropic philosophy. I wanted employees whose professional mission was to go to any length to please the clients who sat in our chairs. I wanted our employees to be trained in technical, personal, and professional skills. But, most importantly, I wanted to use my business as a vehicle to give back to the community and to help those who were less fortunate.

With all of these high ideals spinning around in my head, I still needed to tell Marie about my decision to dissolve our partnership. And, I dreaded the thought of doing it. Marie was my good friend and confidante. Being a business owner wasn't nearly as intimidating when she was there to share the responsibility of running the salon. When things were going badly, we could empathize with each other while putting on our proverbial happy faces for our employees and families.

Even as a number of our stylists came and went, I knew that at least there was one other person who was heavily invested in the salon and wouldn't walk away. There were always two of us to stay after hours, review the day's accounting, or talk over business problems. It was fun and uplifting when we went out for a late dinner at our favorite Italian restaurant down the street. When we got the high-priced check, Marie would always say, "Don't worry, Kay. We work so hard, we deserve this meal." She made me realize that we needed to have fun, too. I would always reply, "You're right, we deserve this!"

With my mind firmly made up, I knew that if I didn't tell Marie about my decision right away, I would literally explode. Early the next day, I met with Marie for our usual morning meeting at the downstairs coffee shop. After the usual chat with my favorite barista, Marie and I sat down at a corner table. I found myself folding and re-folding my paper napkin into smaller and smaller pieces, like a nervous high school girl.

As I looked in her direction, it was obvious to her that I had more on my mind than the day's incoming clients. "Marie," I said, "I want to pursue a new direction for myself. I haven't been happy, and I... I want to break up our partnership."

Startled, she stared at me in disbelief. "What? We're doing so well! We aren't forgoing our own paychecks like most small business owners and we have enough customers to keep us going for a long time!"

"That's the problem," I said, "It can't just be the two of us who are doing well."

Normally soft-spoken, Marie exclaimed, "This is a business! What else matters?"

"The most important people are our employees and the people in the community who need our help," I responded.

Dumbfounded, she replied, "Our employees? They aren't here for our sake, Kay. They come and go so fast at the salon that it is like they are using a revolving door!"

"Of course they do! They don't know any better because we haven't provided any education or a career path for them to succeed. They're doing what they think they're supposed to do, which is making the most money that they can. We watch as they jump from salon to salon to get higher commissions, but they never advance their careers. Our competitors who recruit stylists by offering higher commissions eventually go out of business. I learned in my business classes that if we have a similar wage structure in place, we won't be in business very long either. If we can retain loyal employees by helping them grow in their careers and lives, our business can be a stable partner in our community," I explained. As I blurted this out, I had no idea how to make it work but I knew it had to be done.

By the look on Marie's face, I sensed that she was silently saying to herself, "Does she really know what she's saying?"

In 1982, I bought out Marie's interest in the salon and became the sole owner of Hair on Broadway. At the time, I was excited and nervous, determined and afraid. There were a hundred little things that I had taken for granted when I was part of a team of two. Even though I missed Marie's contributions, for the first time in a long while, I had the freedom of answering only to myself.

For four years, I struggled to work toward my vision of improving employee retention, offering excellent service to our customers, and providing community service.

A well-known clothing consultant in Seattle, Maryann Pember, befriended me and taught me the ropes on how to become a credible entrepreneur. She graciously took me under her wings and showed me how to add some classy touches to my salon with advice such as, "Kay, the paper cups on top of the plastic cones that you use for serving coffee to your customers look tacky. I want you to go out and purchase real glass cups to make your customers feel special. And, when you give your customers a discount on their service say, 'Mrs. Smith, you saved $20 on your service today.' You need to speak up and get out of your shy and humble ways. No one will ever know how lucky they are to have their hair done in your salon unless you tell them."

When I became overwhelmed with all of the changes I had to make, Maryann sat me down and said, "Kay, I am working with you so hard because I believe you have the potential to own the best salon around. You are hard-working, committed, and above all, you have a PASSION for what you're doing. I want to help you make your vision a reality and I believe you can pull it off."

Hearing her words brought back memories of what my Mother told me as a little girl growing up in Japan, "Keiko, of course you can do it. Do you want to know why I say this? Because I know you are different."

Working with Maryann and following her advice over the next several years helped me grow as a business person and also raised the image of my business tenfold. But, with all of this effort to build my business, everything around me seemed to be falling apart. In order to pay the bills, I personally had to produce most of the income to support the overhead for my business. To many of my employees, I was just another person who owned one of the styling chairs next to them. I am sure that some of them didn't trust me.

As a sole business owner, my confidence level finally came to a breaking point one afternoon when I passed by the row of shampoo bowls and chairs. I saw Mrs. Doherty sitting there wiping away the neutralizing solution that was dripping down her face. She cried out, "Can you help me? I'm a dripping mess."

I immediately grabbed a clean towel from the shelf and rushed over to assist her. As I helped Mrs. Doherty pat her face dry, I was embarrassed that this customer was being treated so poorly in my salon.

Apologizing to her profusely, I replied, "I am so sorry that this has happened to you."

In an instant, I rushed into the employee room to find Eugene, the stylist who was performing the perm service for Mrs. Doherty. I found him standing by a wall, talking and laughing on the phone.

I hollered, "Eugene, please get off the phone and pay attention to your customer. The neutralizing solution is running down her face."

Instead of promptly responding to my call, he lingered on the phone for a while longer before hanging up.

"Why are you neglecting your customer? You are being paid a 50% commission for your services, so you should be taking good care of your client," I shouted, angrily.

"No, Kay, you have it all wrong. I'm giving *you* 50% for the services that I perform," he replied, with a cavalier attitude.

I could hardly believe what I was hearing. This unfortunate episode was a reaffirmation that my employees thought *they* owned their own business while working in *my* salon! All my hopes for building the salon of my dreams suddenly went out the window at that moment.

To top things off, the Broadway neighborhood was starting to decline. The once trendy businesses around me were closing their doors one by one. Suddenly, I was surrounded by Pizza Hut and other fast food restaurants. Men wrapped in blankets slept in my doorway and the hallways were littered with trash. My regular customers began to complain.

I had no choice but to put my salon up for sale. Even though I still owed $32,000 of the $40,000 loan from the SBA, I made the painful decision to close the doors to Hair on Broadway and began my search for a new location.

CHAPTER 8:

A NEW DIRECTION

So, there I was. No salon to contribute to my family's livelihood and still deep in debt. It certainly felt like I had hit rock bottom. But, I couldn't take the time to feel sorry for myself. I had work to do and I was determined to make a go of it with a salon at a new location.

The location I found was at 904 Pine Street in downtown Seattle. The name, "Hair on Broadway," I decided, would not work for my new salon. I didn't want to name the salon after myself like "Kay's Hair Design" or use a fluffy female sounding name like "Powder Box." Instead, I wanted a simple name that would attract both women and men. I named my new salon, "Studio 904 Hair Design," a direct reference to its address.

Opening a new salon meant another loan. By this time, I was perceived by lenders as a credible business owner. Having survived eight years in business convinced them that, "This woman must know what she is doing." No matter what they thought, I felt like I was bootstrapping my business every inch of the way. I was happy that the bank agreed to roll the existing loan from my first salon into the new loan and add some additional funds to cover the build-out costs for my new salon. However, even though I had a track record of running a successful business, I had to take a second mortgage on our house before the bank would approve the loan.

There was one more thing I had to do before opening the door to my new salon. I had to solidify a realistic business plan and incorporate specific steps to ensure that the vision I had for my salon, that is, improving employee retention, offering excellent service to my customers, and providing community service, would take hold and thrive. If I didn't put one together, I knew that what had occurred to my salon during the previous eight years would happen all over again. There was no way I was going to allow that to take place.

It was about this time that I came across an industry magazine called *Cutters*, in the middle of a stack of incoming mail. The magazine was from a salon business consulting group all the way across the country in Connecticut. After reading their philosophy of teamwork, hourly pay systems, and training for employees to help them advance up their pay scales, I could hardly believe my eyes! It was like a miracle! What was I waiting for? I decided to travel to Connecticut and learn more about this new approach to salon business management.

I was nervous about making this trip, but I gave myself a pep talk, "Go. This is a golden opportunity for you to grow as a business woman and steer your business in a new direction. It is what you have been longing to do. What's stopping you?"

After spending a week in the countryside of Killingworth, Connecticut, I was amazed and overwhelmed at what I learned about running a salon with a unique culture and strategy. The instructor for Cutter's Business Center was named Joe. He spent eight hours a day for a week with a handful of salon owners from across the country who wanted to learn a new way of doing business.

During our daily sessions, Joe constantly challenged us to break out of the traditional ways we operated our salons. The bantering between Joe and a salon owner went something like this...

Joe: "Why would you want your stylists to call their own shots and do what they, not you, want to do?"

Salon owner: "Because they bring their own clients and my salon needs new clients."

Joe: "You are wrong. It's *your* job to bring in new clients and moreover, it's *your* job to make sure that clients are more than satisfied when they leave your salon. You must take ownership of *your* business!"

Joe: "What would you have to do so that *every* client looks great when they leave your salon?"

Salon owner: "I need to train my stylists to follow customer satisfaction procedures."

Joe: "You are absolutely right. So how would you do that?"

Salon owner: "I can't afford to train every stylist. Besides, they work for themselves on commission or rent one of my chairs. I can't force them to take the training."

Joe: "You are right-on! In order to make this work for the long-term, you need to have your stylists work *for* you. And, you must take on the responsibility of helping them succeed and grow. You have to learn how to manage your cash so you can make payroll in good times and bad times, how to become a good marketer, and how to evolve into being an effective teacher."

"If you can put this whole system together, you will truly have a team of highly skilled stylists working together to please all the clients who come into your salon!" Joe exclaimed, as he drove home the most important points to me and my colleagues.

Joe continued, "Furthermore, you will be doing a great service to individuals entering the cosmetology industry. They will get the training they need and stable pay to begin their careers. The way it is now, new stylists drop out of the industry like flies. Did you know that 80% of stylists leave our industry within the first two years because of financial instability? Some will survive, but "salon-hopping" in search of higher commissions or cheaper chair rental fees will eventually take its toll."

"Yes, and that's the reason why none of us can move forward and keep growing and learning. The way things are now, it's a losing battle for salons, stylists, and our clients," I said.

"Kay, you are absolutely right, Joe replied. "Your job as a salon owner is to create a WIN for the business, a WIN for the stylists, and most importantly, a WIN for your customers."

Even though I learned a lot of business skills and how to think in a new way during that one week training course, I knew I had a lot more to learn. I needed to embrace the concept of "lifelong learning" and to grow and groom myself to be a successful entrepreneur. The training helped me to realize that it was not enough for me to be a good hair stylist, I had to also create an efficiently run operation and incorporate practices that were foreign to most hair salons in the industry. I was scared to my core, and worried about all the changes I had to make.

I remembered how Jean, my first boss, was always in the community recruiting new customers for her salon. If I was to fulfill my vision, I knew that I would have to take on that role. It's an entirely new ball game when a salon does not require its stylists to recruit their own customers and when stylists receive a set salary, regardless of how many clients they see during the day. It would also be my responsibility to make sure that every client was happy with the services they received and left the salon looking their personal best with great haircuts, styles, and colors after every visit. This task would be a big challenge and I asked myself, "Do I have it in me to take on such a monumental project?" I made up my mind and decided that I had to at least give it a try.

I opened Studio 904 Hair Design with four stylists: Rick, Bonnie, George, and Pam. They were excited to be the first in the industry to work for a salon that offered a new way to work. They would not be working on commission; instead, they would have stable, hourly pay with benefits that included vacation pay, medical/vision insurance, and paid training time. The most uplifting change they told me was working in an environment where each member of the team supported and shared their knowledge with each other.

The opening day at Studio 904 Hair Design was filled with laughter and energy. The salon was small and compact and designed in a modern, Italian style. I chose colors of white and pale grey – a more classic look compared to the pop-culture style of the salon on Broadway that had red furniture and chrome track lighting. The more subdued style suited me.

I framed the salon's vision and mission statement on the wall and proudly pointed it out to every guest who came to help us celebrate...

VISION – To be a revolutionary business and create a unique opportunity by improving the quality of life for all the citizens we serve.

MISSION – Innovation, Quality, and Value. We at Studio 904 strive to exceed our customers' expectations.

When leaders in the cosmetology industry heard of my business methods, they told me:

"This won't work. You're trying to swim upstream in a downstream world."

"You will never be able to sell this kind of an approach to stylists. They are used to working for themselves, not as part of a team."

"Customers are not used to working with a team of stylists.

They want the same stylist for life."

"What? You are paying your stylists whether they are busy or not? You'll go broke in no time."

I tried not to let these negative comments get me down. Needless to say, I was very determined to make this new way of operating a salon work and I was especially motivated to show all of the naysayers that I was right.

CHAPTER 9

MIRROR, MIRROR, ON THE WALL

When Joy walked into my salon, she looked like a fashion model. Blond hair fell to her shoulders in soft curls, framing the most perfect facial features and porcelain skin I had ever seen. When I discovered that she was my next client, I instantly froze. What could I possibly do for a woman who was already so perfect?

In the reception area, Joy glanced through one of our hair style magazines. She gave me a warm smile and delivered a soft hand-shake. As I carefully escorted her to the styling chair, I glanced at her stunning face in the mirror. I couldn't help but wonder what it would be like to look even half as beautiful. She probably has the world in the palm of her hands, I thought, as she was undoubtedly presented with more opportunities in her life than the average person. But enough speculating on my part; there was work to do.

"Joy, can you tell me what you are looking for in a style today?" I asked.

She began to speak before I could finish. "I really need help with my hair," she said. "I haven't been happy with it for a long time.

I hate it, actually, and I don't really like how I look when I see myself in the mirror."

I could hardly believe what I was hearing. She looked beautiful to me, even though her hair was now flat and somewhat disheveled.

"Let's talk about how we can find a style you will be happy with," I replied, making eye contact with her in the mirror.

"I want to camouflage my big nose and ears," she complained. "I am so self-conscious of my receding hairline as well. I just don't feel very attractive anymore and I recently noticed that I am beginning to get "crow's feet" around my eyes. Ugh."

"I don't know why I was born with this thin, blond hair," she continued. "I would give anything to have thick, dark hair like yours."

"What are you saying?" I responded, gently. "I think your features are perfect. The curls in your hair provide a nice, soft frame to your face. I can't see any of the flaws you are talking about."

Joy then pulled a small photo out of her designer wallet and showed it to me.

"This is a picture that was taken of me around ten years ago," she explained. "My life was great then. I was on top of the world and I felt pretty every day."

"Is that your husband sitting next to you?"

"Yes," Joy admitted. "I was married to Jeff, but that ended. Unfortunately, our marriage lasted only two years."

As I listened to her story, I didn't know what to say.

"When I turned 32, I began noticing the imperfections in my face. I felt like I was "over the hill," she added. "Then, I lost my job as a receptionist at a law firm. I know that it was because they thought I was getting too old!"

"You are still a beautiful woman," I insisted, unwavering in my perception.

"I would give anything if you could make me look and feel like I did when this photo was taken," Joy said.

Cutting and styling Joy's hair was a major revelation for me. It helped me understand that good stylists need to recognize that they are dealing with a complex human emotion called "self-esteem" as they go about determining the best style and cut for their clients.

When I looked at Joy, I saw a beautiful woman. What she saw in the mirror, however, was a woman who had failed at her marriage and at her work. For most of her life, Joy certainly received special attention because of her extremely good looks. Now, in her mid-thirties, she suddenly found herself feeling that her beauty had faded and she had nothing else to offer the world. She hadn't seen the need to improve her mind or her skills over the years, which led her to becoming an insecure and unhappy person.

Joy's current life situation reminded me of a quote that went something like this: "What you know today is not enough to keep you moving forward." I could feel my Mother's presence and the encouragement she gave me to find meaning in life and to always be open to learning new things.

The most beautiful people in the world will not see themselves as attractive if they lack confidence. As a stylist, a client's self-esteem needs to be the template we use to decide how best to cut and style their hair. After working with Joy, I stopped looking at clients in the mirror to figure out what they might be look like with a new hair cut or color. Instead, I talked to each client to learn more about what was going on in their lives and how they viewed themselves. Over time, as I learned to ask the right questions, I taught my employees how to do the same thing and to appreciate the importance of a client's self-esteem in delivering good customer service. Although this is a simple philosophy, it took one special client to bring it to light. Since then, it has become a hallmark of Studio 904's training and one of the practicing beliefs that make us unique.

CHAPTER 10:

LENDING A HELPING HAND

One day in 1982, Richard, a good client of the salon, had an unusual request for me. He was the director of the Northwest Cerebral Palsy Center in Seattle and an active volunteer in the community. As he looked at his finished haircut, pristine as usual, he said to me, "Kay, I was wondering if you would do me a big favor."

"Sure," I said, "Ask away."

"Would someone from Studio 904 be willing to come to the Center and give haircuts to the young men who reside there?"

"Don't they have someone who regularly cuts their hair?" I asked.

"Well, we do have a few stylists who come and give haircuts, but you should see what they do to our residents. They carelessly buzz off their hair, making them look more disabled. These are young men and they care about how they look. I have been trying to think of a way to get them great-looking haircuts just like the one I got today," said Richard, as he smoothed his hands over his freshly groomed hair.

"Let me see what I can do," I told him.

I asked my staff if anyone would be willing to volunteer at the Center on their day off. No one volunteered, so I decided to go myself. When I pulled up in front of the Center, I was really nervous because I had never done anything like this before. The large, two-story, brick building looked very much like a small hospital and was not very welcoming.

When I opened the front door, I was pleasantly surprised as I was immediately greeted by a friendly receptionist. "You must be Kay. The guys have been waiting for you. They are really excited to get their hair cut." As she pressed one of the numerous buttons on her switchboard, she said, "I'll call downstairs to let them know you're here." She continued, "Walk to the end of the hallway, take a left, and then go down the stairs. You will find them in the room at the foot of the stairs." When I reached the bottom of the stairs, I saw eight young men gathered in a room with a wide, open entry and yellowed walls. Some were in wheelchairs; others were lying on their sides on rolling beds. A damp, musty smell permeated the chipped, linoleum tile floor.

Some of the men were middle-aged, but most appeared to be young adults in their teens or twenties. They greeted me with smiles and sounds that were difficult for me to decipher. Some moved their heads from side-to-side in seemingly random motions; others flapped and flung their hands in excitement, as if to say, "We're glad you're here! We've been waiting for a long time to get our hair cut!"

A woman walked over to me and introduced herself, "Kay, it's so nice to meet you. My name is Sue and I will be your helper today. These guys are really excited because I told them that you will be giving each of them a designer haircut."

As I looked around the room at the eight young men, I realized how challenging it was going to be to cut their hair because most of them were unable to hold their heads up by themselves. Even with Sue's assistance, they often jerked uncontrollably. I was worried that one slip of my scissors would result in a serious injury. The thought of that happening made me very nervous.

Sensing my tension, Sue tried to lighten the mood. She laughed and said, "First in line is David. He has the funniest sense of humor. We nicknamed him "Mr. Ham" because he keeps us laughing with all of his funny jokes. Isn't that so, David?"

David replied by giving me a big grin and belted out a shrieking noise that sounded like, "YEAH!"

He was a handsome, young man with a crop of sandy hair and wore a faded, wash-worn t-shirt with a big logo splashed on the front. Appearing to be about sixteen years old, I said, "Hello David, I'm looking forward to cutting your thick head of hair. I know I can give you a nice style." I sprayed his hair with water while Sue covered his face with a towel. When his hair was thoroughly wet, I began cutting. His head quickly began to jerk back-and-forth. The severity of his movements grew so bad that I couldn't continue with my cutting. Sue used her soothing voice, and as she held his hands, she said "It's okay, David. Now, try to relax. We will be finished soon and then you will be one handsome guy with a new haircut."

When Sue held his head up so that I could cut the hair around the nape of his neck, his neck became wet with perspiration as he struggled to keep his head up. Even with Sue's help and me cutting as fast as I could, it was still an exhausting process for all of us. It made me sad to see this handsome, young man, fighting against every muscle in his body just to hold his neck steady long enough for me to trim his neckline. I thought to myself, "What did this young man do to deserve this life that was so hampered by the debilitating effects of cerebral palsy?"

When I was almost finished with his haircut, I felt a wave of nausea creeping up in my throat. I ran into the nearby restroom and closed the door behind me and quickly found an empty stall. With my head above the toilet bowl, I threw up everything that was in my stomach. When the gagging finally stopped, I flushed the toilet and slowly walked over to the sink, looking at my pale and helpless image in the mirror. I splashed some cold water on my face, looked in the mirror again, and gave myself a pep talk, "Kay, why are you such a weakling? Pick yourself up and go out there with a smile! Give them the best haircuts you can!"

After I completed all the haircuts, I held up a mirror so that each man could see the finished result. Without exception, each young man let out loud cries of happiness and joy. Even though the sounds were mumbled, it definitely seemed to me that they were shouting "I LOVE MY NEW HAIRCUT!" As I stood there and surveyed the entire group, it struck me how handsome they all were. I thought, "Too bad that most of the world will never have a chance to meet them and experience the extreme pleasure they exhibited with such a simple thing as a haircut." Seeing the twisted smiles on these men, as each one thanked me, was enough of a reward for my hard work. As I left the Center, I made a promise to them that I would be back in four weeks to cut their hair again.

I provided these young men with regular haircuts for the next two years. Eventually, some of my staff members came with me. Most came only once, but a few continued for a longer period of time. After I quit going, my guess is that the men went back to having their old buzz cuts. That thought saddened me, but I reminded myself that I had made them happy for two years doing what I did best.

Looking back, I realized that I received a thousand times more from these young men than I ever gave them. They taught me humility, gratitude, and the acceptance of the fate that plays out in our daily lives. Volunteering at the Center was how I began to give back to those in need. Inspired by my initial rewarding experience at the Northwest Cerebral Palsy Center, I implemented a variety of community service programs at Studio 904 to help those whose lives would be positively impacted by a helping hand.

CHAPTER 11:

NO QUICK FIXES

I have attended dozens of industry seminars with titles and taglines written in bold letters like, "Double your Business in an Instant!" And, "How to Attract More Clients Than You Know What to Do With!" One thing they all had in common was the promise to teach you how to bring busloads of clients to your front door. With their "secret" marketing strategies, they claimed that your income and profits would be sky high in a matter of days. It was easy to get caught up in their enthusiastic sales pitches and unsubstantiated expertise.

I had an opportunity to experience for myself what can happen with mass media exposure. Shortly after I moved to Studio 904 on Pine Street, I was invited to appear on a popular, Seattle television show called *Northwest Afternoon* to perform makeovers on several local women. I would be the hair stylist and work alongside a well-known make-up artist who had her own skin care company. At the time, I couldn't have been more excited.

The four participants who were chosen to receive makeovers

came from an applicant pool of more than 100 people from all over the state. They each had a touching, personal story that appealed to the viewing audience.

I was nervous, but exhilarated, as all the pieces of the show quickly fell into place. This was the opportunity of a lifetime to show the world the expert skills in hair design and color that we practiced every day at Studio 904.

Before the show was taped, I met with each of the women at the salon for a hair consultation. I asked them questions like, "Why do you want a makeover? How do you feel about yourself now? What is your vision of the finished look? How much work are you willing to put into your hair maintenance?"

My staff and I listened carefully to each woman's wants and needs. After they were done talking with us, we assembled a written plan of action based on what we thought would complement each of their individual facial features and head shapes.

I spent a lot of time with one of the women, Jody, who was hesitant and insecure about the makeover. She was a small woman with long, light-brown hair that lacked luster. In addition, she had unremarkable facial features and freckled skin.

"I'm a mother of two toddler boys and I live in Bremerton," she told me. "My husband serves in the Navy and he's gone a lot."

"What are you looking for in a makeover?" I inquired, probing for a few more details.

She replied, "I want to bring the romance back to my marriage. It seems like he hardly pays attention to me anymore."

"So, you want to see a dramatic difference in how you look?" I asked.

"Yes, I'm tired of people looking past me and treating me like I'm not even there. When I go to the shopping mall, looking for clothes with my two boys strapped in their stroller, the salespeople treat me like I'm a second-class citizen. They don't even offer to help me," she complained.

"I guess what I'm trying to say," she finished, "is that I want to be noticed. I want to stand out in a crowd."

And so, together, we looked through hundreds of hairstyle photos and picked out several that appealed to her.

We did this with each of the four participants. My team and I sketched out a style that would not only enhance each woman's face, but leave her with the finished look she was dreaming about.

Jody and the other women came into the salon at 7:00 a.m. on the morning that our segment was scheduled to air on television. My staff and I were full of energy, waiting to start with all of the needed hair color products, perm rods, solutions, scissors, blow dryers, and iron curling tools lined up on trays at our stations.

Giggling with shy excitement, Jody was eager to start the beautification process. We gave her a long, layered haircut and permed her hair in spirals around long rods that cascaded down from the top of her head. Next, we applied a golden, copper-toned color that I knew would look ravishing even under the harsh lighting that was used in the television studio. I wrapped Jody's hair up in a towel and walked her over to the make-up artist with a satisfying smile that comes with knowing that you've done a good job.

The entire salon was in a similar mood, filled with light-hearted laughter and grins, as everyone rushed around to finish in time for the show.

We were driven to the television station in specially provided taxis. When we arrived, we quickly went backstage and frantically dried and styled everyone's hair.

Suddenly, I heard the camera crew yell out a five-minute warning while I was fussing around with the last-minute touches to each woman's hair. The next thing I knew, the make-up artist and I were lit up beneath the bright, warm, stage lights. I swallowed hard as I heard the sound of clapping from the audience and we were introduced. I was on live television!

The four makeover participants entered and walked onto the stage, one at a time, as I explained what we had done with their hair and appearance. Each woman had been completely transformed, almost unrecognizable from how she had looked before our in-depth hair and make-up procedures. All four were strikingly gorgeous in their own way.

Jody was the last person to make her way to the stage. My heart made a little leap when she appeared with her long, copper curls bouncing lightly against her shoulders. Her skin was like porcelain and her lips glistened with a soft, coral-colored lipstick.

The audience gave Jody a standing ovation as she walked to the center of the stage with a radiant smile. After her appearance, the show came to a close. I was so relieved that the show had gone well and actually felt like I was "floating." That didn't even come close to the joy I felt, however, when Jody and the others came running up to us to express their gratitude for what we had done for them.

Upon returning to Studio 904 in downtown Seattle, I found the rest of the team bursting with a different kind of excitement.

"Kay, you won't believe this! The minute the show went off the air, our phone started ringing and it hasn't stopped for an hour!" exclaimed Naomi, my front desk coordinator.

It continued to ring for the next week. "I loved the beautiful makeovers you and your stylists did on the *Northwest Afternoon* show," they said. "I want to make an appointment for a complete makeover for myself."

Suddenly, we had more clients than we did chairs in the salon. Women came from all over the city, in twos and in threes, many leaving their baby strollers in our entry way. Every one of my stylists was kept busy all day long, every day.

It was hard to believe. Every time I woke up, I thought that I was dreaming. Happily, there were always customers lined up outside our door when I arrived for work in the morning.

Reality, however, eventually reared its ugly head about two weeks later when our customer count started to drop. Seemingly all at once, the phone calls changed from "I want to make an appointment" to "I want my money back!"

"I demand a refund!" shouted one customer.

"May we ask why? Are you not happy with the new hair color and cut that you received in our salon last week?" The staff was beside themselves, trying to find out what had changed so dramatically.

"I thought I would see a significant change in my life," they exclaimed.

"Your life?" we asked, quizzically.

To a person, they said, "I was expecting my makeover to change how people treat me."

"Are you maintaining your new look at home? Washing, blow drying, and styling your hair the way we showed you?" we asked.

"I don't have time for that! My mornings are busy with getting my kids off to school," they explained.

"I think we pointed out to you the importance of taking care of your hair on a daily basis. So, what I'm hearing is that you've let your hair go?" we asked, as we tried to clarify their concerns.

"I told you already! I don't have that kind of time to spend on myself. My husband still doesn't look at me like he used to. He hardly pays attention to me at all. There haven't been any compliments or signs of affection from him or anyone else! The one thing I know is that I spent $225 in your salon for all that stuff and now I want my money back! Whatever you did, it's not working."

On and on, the complaints kept coming.

Staring helplessly at the phone, I wondered how we could possibly be at fault because these women were unhappy with their lives and their marriages. Because of Studio 904's money-back guarantee policy, however, I had no choice but to agree to the refunds.

We received dozens of similar phone calls in the following weeks from people who expected a sudden change in their lives and fortunes because they had a makeover done in our salon. When that didn't happen, they blamed us. The refunds we ended up giving totaled about 50% of the income we received from the new customers we attracted from our television appearance. It was very depressing.

This experience was a defining moment for me. It taught me not to count on any "get rich quick" schemes with my business. I learned that a horde of new clients chasing the latest fad can quickly disappear.

To me, the moral of this story is to work hard and attract customers who will stay with you for the long haul. Don't market to anyone and everyone. Find a match with people who believe in the same philosophies and lifestyles that you want to cultivate in your business. I found out the hard way. Sadly, my story is one of the marketing lessons that isn't taught at business seminars.

CHAPTER 12:

ONE OF THE WORST
MOMENTS IN MY LIFE

Anthony was a well-known, Minneapolis hair stylist who trained with the acclaimed Vidal Sassoon in England. He was frequently featured in magazines like *Modern Salon* and *Glamour* and knew his way around New York runways and Europe's highest fashion districts. A few times a year, he traveled to Seattle to put on expensive demonstrations for local stylists who were eager to learn about his trendsetting, hair cutting techniques and the newest clothing styles.

In 1982, I took the time to attend one of Anthony's demonstrations at a hotel in downtown Seattle and sat in awe as he performed his magic on a brightly-lit stage. He was tall and self-assured, and wore black leather, Italian-made shoes that clearly stood out on stage. His presence and command of the audience was inspiring and something to watch. As he snipped and flipped strands of hair at lightning speed, I wished that I had that same kind of mastery. When he finished with one of his demonstrations, a young woman with fine, delicate, facial features and long, blond hair confidently walked onto the stage. Her overall presence was so striking that she looked like a professional model.

"What's your name, sweetie?" Anthony asked.

"Claire," she said. Although her appearance was stunning, I detected a hint of nervousness.

Without another word, Anthony wrapped a cape around Claire's shoulders and began his work. In seconds, hair started to fly every which way. I should have been paying closer attention to the cut, but what stood out to me was the scared look on this girl's face. Her shoulders were also rigid and filled with tension.

"Now, watch this," announced Anthony, "You must take complete control over the client and her hair if you want to become a master-level stylist. This is your show! And you must carry out your vision for her head of hair."

"What about what the client wants? Doesn't that matter?" I mumbled to myself, but I didn't have the nerve to speak up and repeat my thoughts in front of the large crowd.

Anthony continued to whittle away at Claire's hair. Every time I thought he was done, he kept on cutting. I could eventually see tears welling up in her eyes and I felt sick to my stomach as I watched how increasingly miserable she became.

When he finally finished, Anthony whipped the cape off of Claire's shoulders as if he was completing a magic trick. He then shouted out to the crowd, "Now, this is what's popular on the fashion runways in New York! Isn't it a gorgeous cut?" The audience surged to its feet and clapped loudly. Feeling trapped by my surroundings, I reluctantly joined in. Out of the corner of my eye, however, I watched as Claire stood up and walked off the stage with a distraught look on her face.

In spite of what I had just witnessed, I arranged for Anthony to give two private classes in my salon the following year. I felt that I had to expose my stylists to his advanced hair cutting techniques and modern fashion sense because I wanted to improve the quality of work at my salon.

Anthony and I kept in touch over the years and one day, in the middle of a hectic afternoon, the receptionist called me over, handed me the phone, and said that Anthony was calling from Minneapolis. We quickly exchanged pleasantries and he hurried to make his point.

"Kay!" he exclaimed, "I have wonderful news! I'm moving to Seattle!"

"What? Is this going to be for good?" I replied.

"Yes, I've been in Minneapolis for five years now and I think it's time for a change. I'll be there next week to start setting things up."

"Wow, so soon," I said, trying to process what he had just told me.

Caught off guard, I was speechless and had no idea what else to say.

"Kay," Anthony continued, "I'm calling you because I want to talk to you about a wonderful business opportunity with me. Can we meet for lunch after I get there? I think you'll like what I'm going to offer you."

I had no clue what Anthony had in mind, but his excitement, which was similar to his presence on stage, was contagious. "Yes! Let's do that!" I agreed.

After he arrived in town, we met at a well-known, upscale restaurant in downtown Seattle. Anthony approached me with the look of some-one who had just walked off the cover of *Gentlemen's Quarterly* *(GQ)* magazine. His dark hair was slicked back with a heavy coating of pomade and his leather jacket looked like a million bucks on top of his tailored, grey wool slacks.

"Can you give us a table in a quiet corner of your restaurant?" he asked the waiter.

We were escorted next to a window in the back and Anthony didn't waste any time in spelling out what he had in mind.

"Kay, thanks for coming. I'm so excited to talk to you about a partnership between the two of us." He was intense with his direct eye contact and animated gestures. "Here is my plan. I'll be completely moved to Seattle in two weeks and I need a salon to call home. I've chosen your salon, Studio 904, as my home base!"

"Uh... Ummm... Why?" I asked, totally taken aback by his plan.

"I realized that there are a lot of nice salons in Seattle, but I think the two of us can help each other become even more successful. You have a beautiful salon and nice clients, but your stylists' work, pardon the expression, sucks! I can give your stylists ongoing training to raise their skills. Can you imagine? You'll have in-house training by Anthony Marciano, a Vidal Sassoon-trained, master hair stylist from Minneapolis. Clients will be busting down your doors in no time because there will be so much publicity."

"Did you say you'll be working in my salon?" I asked. In my disbelief at what I had just heard, it was the only detail that he mentioned that registered with me.

"Yes, but I won't be there all of the time," Anthony said. "I will be busy with press interviews as well as hosting cutting classes and fashion shows whenever I get the chance. But yes, otherwise I will be at Studio 904 serving clients with the rest of your stylists."

"But, where will all of these clients come from?" I asked, as I began to realize that there might be a problem with his proposed arrangement.

"You'll bring clients into the salon through your regular marketing, but then you'll direct them to my chair. Essentially, I want you to give me my own chair so that I can start to establish my business."

"Oh, I see. You want me to rent you a chair. Did you have a rent figure in mind?" I asked, wanting to get the conversation back to a place where I felt a little more in control.

Anthony's impeccable eyebrows shot up. "You really don't get my offer, do you?"

I replied, "Sorry, but I don't understand how this will be a mutually-beneficial, working relationship." I tried to project professionalism, but I felt outclassed and a little dumb for not understanding his proposal.

He gave me an appalled look and raised his voice. "You will charge me nothing for the chair! In exchange for occupying a space in your salon, I will train your stylists to be the best in the city. Don't you get it? My training is worth thousands of dollars. I'm offering that to you absolutely free of charge!" he explained.

I couldn't ignore the feeling that I was being scammed or something pretty close to it. But, on the other hand, I thought, what if I am turning a blind eye to the chance of a lifetime? I had to consider that there might be some merit to his idea. Under his plan, I would get a celebrity stylist who would attract a lot of new clients, train my fledgling staff, and give Studio 904 a prestigious image.

Anthony leaned in closer to me. "Kay, I need to have your answer today. If you agree, then I can begin working in two weeks."

I cleared my throat. It was dry despite having already drained my water glass. "I'll have to think about it," I said, "I don't think I can give you an answer today."

"What is there to think about? You should be ecstatic that I'm giving you this opportunity. You know, I could have picked any of a dozen other salons in Seattle, but I chose yours." he said, emphatically.

I hadn't thought about Claire and her appearance at Anthony's hair cutting demonstration in a long time, but suddenly I couldn't get her distraught face out of my mind. Tightly gripping the sides of my chair, I made a split-second decision like Anthony had requested.

"I'm sorry," I said, "but I can't take you up on your offer. I don't see how this deal can be a win for me."

"How can you say that? It's a fantastic deal for you," he replied, incredulously.

"It doesn't equate to a "win-win." You want to work in my salon with no committed schedule and have me direct my clients to your own chair so you can put money into your own pocket. What this amounts to is paying you to occupy space in my salon and use my clients, but you are providing nothing in return except training for my stylists."

Anthony stood up abruptly. "You are stupid and small-minded!" he yelled. His face was red. "I don't know how you're still in business! The work that comes out of your salon is so bad. How do you ever think your employees are going to improve unless you have someone like me to teach them? Tell me, who is going to be able to do that for you?"

I wanted to crawl into a hole. Anthony was causing a scene and everyone in the restaurant was staring at us.

"I will teach them," I whispered.

"You? Are you kidding? What makes you think you're capable of training anyone? You've never been anywhere. You're just a local stylist!" he shouted.

I quickly stood up.

"Anthony, I'm leaving." I said.

"Besides, you're a woman. You'll never be seen as a Super Stylist!" he said, as he glared at me.

I ran out of the restaurant with tears streaming down my face, feeling like the whole world was watching me stumble out the door.

"You don't have it in you to do it!" I heard Anthony yelling behind me.

I rushed to my car sobbing, achingly crying out almost unintelligibly, "I *know* that I can train them... I *can* and I *will* train my employees... I *can*, I *can*, I *can*..."

Years later, I realized that I had made the right decision as my own training program became well known and successful.

WATCH MY VIDEO:

Chapter 12: The Worst Day of My Life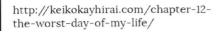

http://keikokayhirai.com/chapter-12-the-worst-day-of-my-life/

CHAPTER 13:

A CRUEL SURPRISE

Looking back, I am amazed that I was able to land on my feet after that demoralizing encounter with Anthony. His reaction, however, was pretty typical within the industry. Male stylists projected themselves as authority figures and used their showmanship to convince female clients of their superiority when it came to fashion and style. That terrible episode and the prevailing attitude toward women in the workplace made me more determined than ever to not only survive, but to also grow my business. The desire to push forward and my passion to build a business that I could be proud of was all the motivation that I needed to continue working ten-hour days at the salon and attend business courses in the evenings to develop my entrepreneurial skills.

I knew that I was on the right track with one of my new strategies as I consistently received feedback from my four stylists about how they enjoyed receiving their weekly paychecks without having to worry about the erratic commission pay system that was standard in the hair salon industry.

It was like music to my ears, for example, when I overheard a client interacting with one of my stylists and ask: "So, George, do you enjoy working here?"

"Yes, I sure do, Mrs. Cohen. I like not having to recruit my own clients. Plus, I can always count on receiving a regular paycheck and benefits each week. Kay provides us with a lot of on-the-job training to keep our hair designs current and she also shows us how to work as a team."

"Isn't that unusual in the salon business?" she asked.

"Yes. Unlike other salons, we aren't paid for how many clients we go out and get. Instead, our wage increases are based on how well we improve on the skills it takes to please our customers."

Another one of my strategies was to introduce a number of innovative salon promotions, such as opening the salon in the evenings to put on fashion shows to benefit a charitable organization, providing "Improving Your Self-Image" classes to nurses at Swedish Hospital, and working with small business owners to provide their employees with tips on how to fix their hair and make-up. It was important to me to tie these promotions into some type of community service. With each promotion, I organized, I felt I was taking a major step toward growing my salon into a socially-responsible business.

Everything was going well until early one morning in January, 1986. On that day, I decided to arrive at the salon a little early so that I could open my mail and organize the monthly bills. I looked at the tall stack of mail on my desk in the back room of the salon and took a deep breath before I began the task of opening each envelope. While sipping a cup of strong, dark coffee that I had just brewed, I instantly felt at ease and murmured to myself, "It's such a nice day. I hope there won't be any surprise invoices for me to pay this morning." As usual, cash was tight and so I often had some anxious moments when I opened my mail.

Among the pile of letters, bills, and advertising flyers, I noticed an official looking envelope that was addressed to: "Kay Hirai, Studio 904 Hair Design." The return address read: "King County Metro." King County Metro is the official name for the public transportation system that serves our county. I wondered why I would be receiving a letter from them and quickly opened the envelope. Pulling out a neatly folded sheet of paper with the King County Metro letterhead at the top, I started reading...

"We want to inform you that the building where you reside, 904 Pine Street, has been chosen as the official site for a new bus terminal serving the cross-town underground bus system...This new transportation route will begin at Union Station near the International and Pioneer Square Districts and end at a location near 904 Pine Street... The demolition date for the 904 Pine Street building has been set for April 12, 1986. All businesses located in this building must be completely vacated well before the date of the demolition... Metro will assist you during your move. To find out how we can assist you with your move and the build-out costs for the new location that you have selected for your business, please attend the public meetings that will commence this month..."

The letter hit me like a ton of bricks. "What? This must be a joke, it can't be true!" I shouted, to no one in particular. My stomach began churning and I literally felt sick. The County is giving me only a three-month notice! They obviously didn't care that I had built my salon only a year-and-a-half ago and that I was just getting started in building my client base. "This simply can't be true!" I told myself, while trying to calm my now visibly shaking body.

When my landlord's office opened at 9:00 a.m. that morning, I grabbed the phone and called them. Sherry, their office manager picked up my call. "Hello, this is Sherry with Landmark Properties," she answered, in a cheery voice.

"Hi, Sherry. This is Kay Hirai from Studio 904, a tenant in your building on Pine Street."

"Oh yes, Kay, how may I help you?" she asked.

"Are you aware that King County Metro plans to demolish the building on April 12th?" I asked.

"So, you received a letter already? she asked, incredulously.

"Yes, just this morning. I am pretty sure that all of the tenants in your building will be receiving this same letter today or very soon. Tell me this is not true. Is this a joke?" I asked.

"I'm afraid it *is* true and the letter you received *is* for real," she responded.

"Sherry, surely your owner must have known about this. He built this brand new, state-of-the-art building only two years ago, just so that he could be bought out by King County Metro and make a substantial profit in the process?" I asked.

"I'm sorry I am not qualified to answer that question," she replied.

"And he got all of us tenants to sign leases, knowing this was going to happen?" I asked, in an even louder tone.

There was complete silence on the other end of the line...

"Oh, I get it. The more tenants he has in the building, the more he will be able to get for it!" I shouted.

"I'm sorry, I don't know what you're talking about," she replied, meekly.

"Sherry, I'm not stupid!" I continued, "There are eight small businesses in this building and we are all being evicted! I'd like to talk to the head person in your organization! And, NOW!"

"I'm sorry he is not available right now," she responded.

I hung up the phone, my head spinning. This sort of confrontational behavior was certainly not like me. I am usually a person who can hold back any fits of rage, but this was too much to take in at one time and so unexpected.

As I sat back to fully absorb what was happening, I remembered what the glossy, promotional flyer from the Small Business Administration had stated: "SMALL BUSINESSES ARE THE BACK-BONE OF OUR ECONOMY. THEY HIRE 60% OF AMERICA'S WORKFORCE. FOR THIS REASON, OUR GOVERNMENT IS WILLING TO PROVIDE HELP TO THE SMALL BUSINESSES OF AMERICA."

Was I really so naïve to believe that propaganda? This sure didn't feel like my government cared much about small businesses. Because we are small, does that make it easier for them to shove us around? There were so many thoughts, questions, and emotions running through my mind after that phone call. The difficult part was that I didn't have any satisfactory answers to calm my anxiety.

Just then, the phone rang. I thought for sure that it was going to be the head of the property management company that I had just called. As it turned out, it was worse.

"Hello, this is Kay," I answered, trying to calm my shaky voice.

The man on the phone yelled, "Kay, "What the HELL IS GO-ING ON? I read in this morning's Seattle Times paper that King County Metro will be demolishing your building on 904 Pine Street so that they can build a new bus terminal!"

It was my banker, Mr. Smith. Oh no, I thought. Mr. Smith was yelling so loudly into the phone that I thought my eardrums were going to burst.

"Yes, that's true, Mr. Smith. I just received a letter from Metro this morning," I whispered.

Mr. Smith immediately responded, "We need our money back! The entire $150,000 that I lent you! The loan needs to be paid back IMMEDIATELY! Do you understand me? I have nothing to show for the loan that I personally approved for you so that you could build your new salon at 904 Pine Street. It will be going up in smoke in three months. I'll be in big trouble with my superiors. Do you understand that I could lose my position with this bank if your loan isn't paid back? Do you realize how serious this is?"

I was absolutely speechless.

"Kay, I want to see you in my office today," he said with a demanding tone.

"Yes... sure," I replied, not knowing what else I could say at the time.

The rest of the morning was a complete blur.

I knew that I had to quickly get a hold of Mr. Lagerquist, my attorney. He was the one person who didn't intimidate me. I always felt comfortable knowing that he did not have an office located in any of the tall buildings in the high-brow financial district of downtown Seattle. Instead, his office was on the second floor of a small office building located on Capitol Hill, a fairly modest neighborhood on the outskirts of downtown.

After making a hasty appointment, he was waiting for me with his usual "big brother" smile when I entered the office.

"Kay, what is going on? he asked. You sounded absolutely frantic when you called my office."

I broke out in tears before I could sit down. In between sobs, I managed to tell him about the Metro letter that I received. Recognizing my distress, he darted out of the office and came back with a glass of cold water and a box of tissues and handed them to me.

"Kay, try to calm down and tell me again what you just said. Better yet, did you bring the letter so that I can take a look at it?" he asked.

After he heard my story, he read the letter. After a minute, he said in his calm, reassuring voice, "I can tell this is devastating news for you. The letter is official. The 904 Pine Street building *will* be demolished."

"But it is so disheartening to think that people take advantage of small business owners in this way," I tried to reason with him. "Big companies do it for the money and the government doesn't seem to care, even though they make all these claims and promises to help us."

"I'm afraid that it is tough for the little guys. Small businesses just don't have the clout that big businesses do," he responded.

"What can I do now?" I asked.

"Kay, this is what you *have* to do. Just suck it up and move forward. You have to protect your salon, your employees, and your customers and make sure that this transition goes as smoothly as possible. You've worked too hard to achieve your vision; you *can't* let this stop you. It may not be as bad as you think because this letter says that Metro will reimburse you for the move as well as the build-out costs for a new salon. You can stall the bank for a little while. In fact, I will give them a call and try to calm them down," he said reassuringly.

"Mr. Lagerquist, where did I go wrong? I've worked so hard to keep everything going in my new salon. What more could I have done?" I asked, waiting to hear a comforting answer.

"Unfortunately, it takes more than hard work to stay in business. A small business owner has to spend just as much time keeping an eye out for economic changes in the city, county, and state. I know that is a lot to ask, but it's the reality of a successful business owner. My advice is not to be such a trusting person in the future," he advised.

I nodded my head, trying to absorb all that he was telling me.

"Kay, you were raised in Japan. Remember the way of the Samurai warriors. They walked with their eyes looking straight ahead but were always ready at a moment's notice to pull out their swords to protect themselves from their enemies," he said with a warm smile. "Now, get busy and go on the hunt for that new location to build your next salon!"

Even though I was upset and shaken, I walked out of his office, ready to face the challenges that lay ahead of me. I was thankful that Mr. Lagerquist was my attorney. He was always there to help me see things in a positive light. As a result, I made a couple of promises to myself after this meeting. One was that I would try to be more like him as I moved forward to build my next salon. Second, and equally important, I was going to help others see the positive side of life when they experience disappointments. It was the least I could do for receiving such valuable advice from a trusted adviser.

CHAPTER 14:

MY PAINFUL GOODBYE

The next three months were incredibly busy for me and the seven small business owners who were located at 904 Pine Street. The other businesses that flanked my salon were small architectural, accounting, and insurance companies. Unlike me, they did not have nearly the amount of money invested as I did in tenant improvements. My salon had been beautifully designed with a built-in reception bar, styling stations, mirrors, shampoo bowls, cabinets, and customized track and wall lighting.

The county's transportation project didn't target just the businesses in our building for relocation. Cafes, gift stores, and numerous other mom and pop businesses within a four-block radius of our building also shared the chaos that was created by this major project. Sidewalks, for example, were blocked off, making it difficult for the public to access these businesses.

After days of waiting, a notice finally arrived, announcing that a meeting would be held the following week to address the concerns of business owners who were being displaced. When I walked into the meeting room in one of the government buildings on Second Avenue the next week, I saw my fellow business owners and a group of interested citizens. The mood was quiet and gloomy. Three official-looking people sat facing us, two men and one woman.

One of the men walked up to the microphone, coughed, and began the meeting.

"Good evening. My name is Mike Hall, and I am the community liaison from King County Metro. To my right is Jim Wright, the head of our construction project team and Helen Odell, who is our business re-location specialist."

Mike gave us an overview of the entire bus tunnel project and explained how it would improve the public transportation system between Seattle's International District and the downtown core. Next up was Jim. He gave a report detailing all of the construction activities and the targeted dates for the completion of each phase.

The last person to speak was Helen Odell. Dressed in a tailored jacket and well-tailored slacks, her short-cropped, sandy hair and face devoid of make-up, gave me the feeling that she was a "no-nonsense" type of woman who was totally focused on getting the task done.

Helen began speaking, "I'm the person most of you will be working with in the coming weeks. It is important that we keep the lines of communication open so that I can assist you each step of the way. My intention is to make your move as smooth as possible with very little effort on your part."

A man in the audience raised his hand. When called upon, he asked, "Helen, so we can call on you anytime when we need help?"

"Absolutely. Metro has committed to paying your moving and build-out costs in full. In other words, you will be fully compensated for any costs you might incur because of the move. You will need to send me all of your invoices from contractors and movers and I'll make sure that checks are sent to them to pay for their services. Oh, one thing I almost forgot to mention. You must get three bids from your contractors and vendors for every part of the moving and build-out process. We will only reimburse you for the contractor or vendor who submits the lowest bid."

I raised my hand and asked, "You mean three bids for everything that will need to be done? That's going to be a lot of work, isn't it?"

"Yes, it will be. But, that is what Metro is requiring you to do," Helen said with a strident voice.

During the months that followed, many businesses were unfortunately forced to close their doors because of the lack of foot traffic. Luckily, my salon's clients were loyal and supported us by making their way around the numerous sidewalk barricades before entering through our front door.

It was sad for me to say farewell to the owners and staff of the businesses that I had frequented and with whom I had become close. For some reason, I felt personally responsible for what was happening to them. I was especially fond of Mary, who owned a small coffee shop on the next block. Almost every day, I stopped there for coffee, pastries, or a sandwich. It felt good to patronize her business and help her out because I knew that she was a single mother with a young son. I gave her a lot of advice on where she could go to learn more about how to operate a business and even helped her obtain a small loan through the Minority Business Development Center, which was located nearby on 16th and Jackson Street.

"Mary, you have such a wonderful café. Isn't it possible for you to just hang on until this construction is over?" I pleaded.

"Making ends meet is tough enough when things are normal," she responded. "Now I'm faced with only a trickle of customers coming in. I can't keep going on like this. Besides, the disruption caused by the bus tunnel construction won't be over in just three months. I'll be struggling with this mess long after you leave the area."

Oh, how I wished the County would take on the responsibility of protecting fledgling business owners like Mary. It just wasn't fair.

Aside from all that was going on around me, I knew I had to secure a lease for my new salon in a yet-to-be determined new location. The Pioneer Square area looked pretty interesting to me. It was in the throes of being renovated and gentrified with an innovative neighborhood revitalization program. What was once considered the skid road of Seattle, with old, shabby buildings, was slowly evolving into office spaces for forward-thinking architects, law offices, graphic design firms, and small theaters.

I remember seeing and liking a building called Merrill Place. It was located on the corner of First Avenue and Jackson streets, only a block away from the nearby waterfront. My husband, Tommy, who owned a small silk screen company, conducted business with many of the graphic design companies in the area. He invited me to attend a grand opening for an up-and-coming graphic design firm located on the fifth floor of the newly remodeled Merrill Place building. I was in awe of this magnificent building, which was recently landmarked as the oldest building in this historic district.

As we rode the elevator to the fifth floor, I said to Tommy, "Wow, I love this building. It's so old, but so contemporary at the same time. Maybe one day, I will have a hair salon in this building."

Things were getting a little tense. I was only a month away from the proposed demolition date of my old salon and I still hadn't found a new location. One late afternoon, however, my real estate agent, who had been furiously trying to find a new location for me, called and gave me the good news.

"Kay, the building you like, Merrill Place in Pioneer Square, has a first floor, corner space that just became available," she said, excitedly.

"Are you sure? Isn't the high-end European furniture store there?" I asked.

"I just got the news that the furniture store closed! In the middle of the night, the owners moved everything out. When morning came, the landlord was shocked to see an empty store because the owners had a lease for two more years."

"So, does this mean the space is up for grabs to new tenants?" I asked.

"Yes. I was there a few hours ago, checking out the space and the area, and I think that it would be a perfect spot for you. I saw many well-dressed, professional men and women walking and shopping in the businesses nearby. Aren't you looking for that type of clientele? I think the area needs a salon like Studio 904 and I think you would be a big hit there," she said, enthusiastically.

"Okay, I'll go there and take a look today. I'll let you know what I think," I replied, with a big smile on my face.

The Pioneer Square area is located just a few blocks west of where one of the new underground bus tunnel terminals would be located. This large terminal would open after the terminal at the north end of downtown (the location of my current salon) was completed. After going through the turmoil at the other end, I felt completely safe building a new salon at this location because I knew that the entire tunnel project would soon be completed.

Walking three blocks east from the Merrill Place building was the heart of the International District, with busy streets lined with Asian restaurants and gift stores. A definite plus, being so close to another bustling business area. I knew this area well. As a teenager, I spent lots of time in the International District visiting my friend, Janet, who lived there.

As I looked around the Pioneer Square neighborhood, I was excited and intrigued by what I saw. I loved the art galleries, restaurants, artist's lofts, boutiques, and gift stores. They were decorated in a way that created an ambiance with an "organic feel" – a melting pot of old and new. There was a diverse group of fast-walking men and women who seemed to be racing toward their destinations, while at the same time, avoiding eye contact with the homeless people who frequented many of the streets in the neighborhood.

There were people who looked like artists, dressed in jeans and t-shirts. And, there were others who looked like architects dressed in fine-woven cotton, pin-striped shirts and neatly pressed, khaki pants. What caught my eye, though, were all of the fashion-forward women dressed in edgy and creatively-designed clothing. They looked like gallery owners, graphic designers, and interior decorators. I wondered where they purchased their clothes, certain that they hadn't bought them in the traditional department stores of downtown Seattle.

In spite of all my enthusiasm, I suddenly felt a strange sense of inferiority. Would my salon, Studio 904, really fit in with the vibe found in the Pioneer Square district? Would the people accept us? Is our work innovative enough to please them? I knew if I wanted to succeed here, I would have to step up our marketing image and pro-duce high-quality advertising materials to attract potential clients who lived and worked in Pioneer Square.

After a lot of thought and advice from others I trusted, I decided to give it a try and signed the lease to open my new Studio 904 Hair Design on the corner of First Avenue and Jackson streets in the Mer-rill Place building.

A month later, on April 12, 1986, the beautiful building located at 904 Pine Street was demolished and quickly flattened by the demolition crew. My heart still aches when I think about that day. What a shame that a new building was torn down so soon after it had been painstak-ingly built. More personally, I felt the same way about my beautiful salon, which I designed and built with attention to every detail. What a waste to be taken away from me after only a year-and-a-half of enjoying its sophisticated atmosphere and supportive clients.

CHAPTER 15:

PIONEER SQUARE, HERE I COME

There I stood. My salon had vanished in just a matter of minutes and my employees were terrified and scattering in all directions. Even my loyal customers were wondering where to go for their next haircut.

Construction on the new Studio 904 Hair Design salon at the corner of First Avenue and Jackson streets in Pioneer Square was slow to begin. Having to get three bids for each job was time consuming and prolonged the process. Even after I turned in my bids to Helen Odell, Metro's project manager, it took a while for her to let me know whether my requests were approved. I was constantly on pins and needles knowing that every delay could jeopardize the July 9th opening date for my new salon.

Helen's phone calls were important, so I made sure that I was always available to receive them. Her calls usually went something like this, "Kay, I received the bids for the drywall job in your salon. They are on the high side for doing that type of work. Can you get someone to give you a lower bid?"

I'm sure she heard my exasperated sigh coming as I replied, "I don't know how I can get a lower bid. All the contractors know what happened to me and are aware that I am on an extra-tight timeline to complete the work. They all act like they are doing me a big favor when I ask them for a bid."

"Okay, she replied. "Just turn in one more bid and I will pay the contractor with the lowest bid."

I felt powerless. Frequently on edge, I wanted to scream, "Why are they putting me through such agony? I didn't ask for this! *They* are the ones who imposed this great inconvenience on me!"

Richard and Misty were the two employees who decided to stay on with me until the new salon opened. The rest of the stylists hurriedly left the salon. I couldn't really blame them. After all, they needed to pay their bills. I was so thankful for Richard and Misty's loyalty, but how could I continue to pay them after the salon closed when I had no revenue coming in? Until the new salon was ready for customers, I had to quickly find a way to serve our clients.

After a little brainstorming, an idea popped into my head. I called Tim, a colleague and a friend. Tim operated a salon on the tenth floor of a downtown building with his partner, Ryan. I asked him if he would consider renting his salon space to me on the days and times that his salon was closed. He was closed on Sundays and Mondays, so he agreed to let me use his space during those days for what I thought was a pretty reasonable fee. Upon hearing the good news, I replied, "Oh, Tim, you are a definite life saver. I'll never forget what you've done for me as long as I live."

"Are you sure about that? Okay. I might call on you when I get displaced and need a place to work. Is that a deal?" he replied, in his usual mild-mannered and humorous way.

I immediately began making phone calls to our loyal clients and told them of my plan. Instead of grumbling, a typical response went something like this, "Kay, what an innovative idea. You are a survivor, aren't you? Of course, I will come to your new, temporary location. Just let me know when you can schedule me." It made me feel good that so many customers were willing to go out of their way to help me out.

At that moment, I realized how loyal these customers were to me and my business. My heart was filled with gratitude and thankfulness to have these wonderful people in my life. It brought back something that I learned in one of my business classes... "A good entrepreneur not only hires qualified employees, but also recruits 'qualified' customers into their business."

It was real work going up the elevator to the tenth floor to set up my temporary salon. On Sundays, I lugged boxes filled with hair blowers, iron curlers, combs, brushes, shampoos, capes, and more. Richard and Misty were both good sports and helped me in any way that they could. We all worked hard on those two-day work weeks at the temporary location, squeezing in every possible customer we could. Fortunately, I was able to bring in enough income during that time to pay my two loyal employees.

"Kay, I've stalled the banker as long as I can. Now, it's time for you to step up and resolve this matter. The bank is threatening to repossess your house if the $150,000 you owe is not taken care of soon," said Mr. Lagerquist, my attorney, on the other end of the phone line.

"Oh, I have so much going on right now. I don't know if I can handle another stressful encounter," I whined.

"I remember you told me that your husband, Tommy, has a friend whose sister is a loan officer at Washington Mutual Bank. Can he get you an introduction to this sister of his?"

"Well, it's not that Tommy really knows her that well. He only plays golf with her brother," I replied, hesitating.

"Does Tommy have a good relationship with the brother?" Mr. Lagerquist asked.

"Oh, yes. Tommy is well-liked by all his friends," I replied.

"Good. That means that you have a connection to the sister who is the loan officer. It's helpful if you have a personal connection with the lender. Now, what you need to do is to meet her and ask her to take over the loan from your existing bank by transferring it to her bank," explained Mr. Lagerquist. In a serious tone, he continued, "This is your only chance. Now don't be shy and don't make excuses. Just go and see if you can get an appointment with her, okay?" Although he couldn't see me, I nodded my head in agreement. "Tell her your unfortunate story, but let her know that Metro will be paying you back for the new salon. You'll be back in business in no time," he concluded.

Mr. Lagerquist was right! Three weeks after my initial meeting with the loan officer, I was informed that Washington Mutual would take over my existing bank loan of $150,000. "Yippee! My house is safe!" I hollered and screamed and literally jumped for joy after I hung up the phone. Even though I was alone in my office, I wanted everyone to hear about my good fortune.

Receiving this good news gave me the energy to continue with my move to Pioneer Square. One important thing I learned from this episode is that it always helps if you are well-liked and respected by the people in the community where you live and work. At desperate moments, you are forced to consider every resource that might be able to extend a helping hand.

An abrupt phone call from the signage company's accounting office interrupted my otherwise calm morning.

"Ms. Hirai. I'm Loretta from Cascade Signs. I'm calling you because it's been over a month and we haven't received payment for the window signs we installed at your salon," she said, using a stern, business-like voice.

"Are you sure? You should have received your payment from Metro by now. Helen, their business relocation specialist, told me a few weeks ago that your invoice was approved and that a check would be sent out within a week," I replied.

"I'm positive that no check has been received by our office in the last week or so," she replied.

"I'm sure that we can straighten this out. I will give Helen a call and get right back to you," I assured her.

This was very worrisome for me because I always try to do my best to pay my bills as soon as they arrive. I immediately dialed Helen's number after I finished my conversation with Loretta. Although I was redirected several times by different recordings, I finally reached Helen's extension number. Her voice recording explained that she was working out in the field and that she would get back to me at her earliest convenience. Helen did not call me back that morning, so, later that afternoon, I called her again. I received the same recorded message. By the end of the day, I still hadn't received a phone call back from Helen.

After three days and still no response from Helen, I called Mike Hall, Metro's community liaison officer whom I had met a few months back at the first public meeting about the project. Luckily, I was able to reach him on the phone.

"Hello Mr. Hall, this is Kay Hirai, the owner of Studio 904 Hair Design, I said. "I hope you remember me. I am the owner of one of the businesses that is in the process of relocating and I am building a new salon in Pioneer Square." Although I wanted to use my strong and self-assured voice, it came out sounding hesitant and meek. For what Metro was putting me through, I wished that I could have angrily shouted at him to make my points.

"Yes, I know who you are. How can I help you?" he asked.

"I am starting to get calls from my contractors who have done work building my new salon. They are asking for their invoices to be paid. In fact, some of them are getting downright hostile and told me that I need to pay them NOW. I've put in numerous phone calls to Helen Odell, but she hasn't returned any of my calls for the last three days," I explained.

"Oh, yes. That is because she is no longer working for Metro," Mr. Hall replied.

"What? What happened to her? She didn't inform any of us that she was leaving," I said, trying to restrain myself.

He cleared his throat and answered, "Well, she *did* leave us rather abruptly."

"Who will be taking over her position as Metro's business relocation specialist?" I asked.

"Kay, we are in the midst of a re-organization and are trying to get back on track. The new person we hire will be in touch with you soon," he explained.

"Soon? I have a lot of contractors on my back. They want to get paid. And they want to get paid yesterday," I said, with emphasis.

"Yes, I understand your frustration. Again, let us do our job and you will hear from us shortly," Mr. Hall replied. The tone in his voice signaled to me that this was the end of our conversation.

Without wasting a minute, I picked up the phone and called Don, a business owner who operated a picture framing shop in the same 904 Pine Street building where I used to have my salon. He had just had an open house to celebrate the opening of his new store in a new space about six blocks north of our old location. I began telling Don exactly what was happening to me during the building process in my Pioneer Square location.

"Don, I don't understand. What do you think is going on with

Metro? I don't know how much longer I can continue to stall my contractors. They are getting pretty angry," I said, looking for a little sympathy.

"Kay, I am lucky that all of my relocation costs have already been covered 100%. I was thinking of you when I heard the rumor that Helen Odell was in trouble and again when she was let go from the project," he said.

"What? You heard this news? I didn't hear a thing." I responded.

"Please don't repeat what I'm about to tell you because it may be just a rumor. Can you promise me that?" he asked.

"You can trust me. I won't say anything, but please tell me," I pleaded.

"Well, this is what I heard... Helen so mismanaged the construction money that the compensation funds were depleted. She went overboard helping some of her friends, so the end result is that people like you, who were at the end of the relocation list, are out of luck as far as getting their contractors paid. I was lucky because I was one of the first ones to find a new location. As a result, I was able to receive funds immediately so that I could build my business."

"So you have been reimbursed for *all* of your relocation costs?" I asked.

"Yes. I am really happy because my new shop was designed and built to better fit my needs."

I started to get that gnawing feeling again in the pit of my stomach. How much more bad news could I handle? Will this ever end? I felt hopeless, forlorn, and destitute – all at the same time. What was worse is that I was dreading the thought of having to go home and tell my husband the latest dose of bad news. I felt terrible for dragging my husband and kids into this downward spiraling mess.

Did I get myself in over my head by attempting this move? Was I a complete failure? Who was I to think that I could survive in this dog-eat-dog world of business? All these questions swirled through my mind, making me doubt myself and what I was trying to do.

At this point, I knew there were only two choices for me. One, I could give up and declare bankruptcy, which would have meant losing everything my husband and I had worked for, including our house. The second choice was to suck it up and borrow more money to finish the construction of my new salon. If I was successful in raising the money I needed, I could at least open my business and start earning some income.

I decided to persevere and move ahead.

My immediate challenge was to pay the numerous contractors who were working to finish up their respective parts of the new salon. I swallowed my pride and asked for help from people who were close to me. My brother-in-law, cousin, and a few close friends generously lent me various amounts of money that allowed me to pay off my current debts.

But that wasn't nearly enough to completely open my new business. I made desperate phone calls to my three largest contractors. After explaining my predicament, I asked each of them if they would consider an extended payment plan. I reassured them that I would be able to make the monthly payments as soon as my salon opened. Surprisingly, they all agreed. Humbled and grateful that they trusted me, I still think of them as my guardian angels.

One big hurdle remained. I was determined to continue negotiating with Metro to get compensated for all of my relocation expenses. There was no way that I was going to let them out of their promise to pay the moving and build-out costs for all the small business owners who were forced to move. Their words at the initial meeting with us kept ringing in my ears. I distinctly remember Helen Odell enthusiastically saying, "Absolutely, Metro has committed to pay *all* of your moving and build-out costs *in full*. You will be compensated for *all* of the costs you incur because of the move."

At this point, I was certain that whatever I needed to do to hold Metro accountable would be completely out of my league. I could see myself getting eaten alive by Metro's attorneys if I tried to go down that road by myself. As a result, I scheduled another visit with Mr. Lagerquist, my always wise and down-to-earth attorney. I knew that he would have some good ideas on to how to deal with this situation.

After outlining some of the key details of my issues with Metro, he said "Kay, there is one thing you might want to do. You can go after Metro with a litigation procedure."

"Litigation procedure? What is that?" I asked.

"It means filing a lawsuit against Metro for their unfair treatment of you. It's a long, drawn-out hearing process, but it basically boils down to your word against theirs," he explained.

"It sounds scary," I replied.

"You won't be doing this yourself. If you decide to go this route, you will have to find an attorney who specializes in litigation work to help you," he said.

"Who would that be? I asked.

"I know a very good attorney, Mr. Bryan Mar. He is of Chinese descent and is very good at what he does. I will give him a call and set up an appointment for you to have a consultation meeting with him," he said.

I rode the elevator up to the 22nd floor of a high-rise building in downtown Seattle and entered the ostentatious-looking entrance of Mr. Mar's office. With its expansive views of Puget Sound, I instantly knew that Mr. Mar's law services would not be cheap.

Mr. Mar was a moderately-built man with a thick head of black hair. His guarded and formal mannerisms made me a bit uncomfortable, but once he started to talk, I knew he would be very thorough and competent in the litigation process. The only question I had was whether I could afford to pay for his services. As though he read my mind, Mr. Mar addressed my concerns by explaining, "Kay, let me tell you how this will work. If you decide to hire me as your attorney, I will not charge you anything for my services if we lose. However, after reviewing the documents of your moving records and the paperwork from Metro, I personally feel that you have a very strong case."

"So you won't charge me a penny if we lose?" I asked, incredulously.

"Yes, that's correct. But if we win, my fee will be 40% of the money you receive from Metro. Does this sound like a plan that will work for you?" he asked.

I did a quick calculation in my head. Even though his fee was enormous, I knew that I had to see this to the end.

"Yes, Mr. Mar. I'd like you to be my attorney and I would like you to file a lawsuit against Metro," I said, trying to sound enthusiastic.

Going through this litigation process was one of the most taxing times in my business journey. In addition to all the stresses involved in opening my new salon, I began the process of battling one of the largest governmental agencies in the City of Seattle and King County.

The litigation process was scary and intimidating. I rehearsed my lines for hours before each trial date and followed Mr. Mar's advice and instructions.

"Kay, just remember to project confidence when you answer the attorney's questions. The worst thing you can do is to come across as meek or scared. Answer the questions directly without mincing your words. Be forceful with what you are demanding. After all, they are the ones who backed out of the deal that was promised to you and not the other way around," he explained. I nodded my head in response, swallowed hard, and took a deep breath before entering the trial room. "Furthermore, be clear with what you are asking them to do for you. Your new salon ended up costing you $180,000. They have paid you only $42,000 so far. They owe you another $138,000. Keep these numbers straight and demand the $138,000 and look directly at them. Do you understand?"

After testifying on trial dates that were set by Metro over a four-month period, Mr. Mar informed me that Metro had agreed to pay the entire $138,000 that was owed to me. When I heard the news, it was one of the happiest days of my life. I felt a strong sense of accomplishment as well as relief. Justice had actually been served to a fledgling, small business owner.

In the end, I paid Mr. Mar his 40% share of the settlement for his work. I kept the remaining 60% to pay back the loans given to me by friends and family, as well as to settle some of the outstanding debt owed to a few contractors. Although I still had a shortfall of $55,000, I was able to move forward with my business and make monthly payments to pay off the remainder of my debt.

I received the Mayor's Small Business Award shortly after the lawsuit with Metro was settled. The award was in recognition for surviving the struggles that I went through in re-establishing my salon in Pioneer Square.

A year later, I introduced a successful proposal to the Washington State Legislature, which provided that no small business be burdened by paying attorney fees when they are pursuing litigation against a government entity for any wrong-doing that negatively impacts their business.

CHAPTER 16:

I DID IT MY WAY... THE KAIZEN WAY

As the opening day for the Studio 904 salon in Pioneer Square drew closer, I had much to do to get ready. The architect suggested a vertical, black canvas banner with our salon name in bold, white, block lettering to go along with the salon's clean and simplistic theme that I had envisioned. He said that the ideal place would be on the exterior wall facing First Avenue. Initially, I was taken aback when I first stood outside and looked at the banner that read "STUDIO 904 Hair Design" because its appearance was so stark against the original, exposed brick walls and the enormously high, wood ceiling. After looking at it for a few minutes, however, I saw how it caught people's eyes as they walked passed the salon. Many of them dropped in to see what we were all about. I was elated; I had never had a lot of walk-in traffic at any of my other salon locations.

When visitors came in to the salon, they were immediately met with a large sign encased in a black frame that was mounted on the entryway wall:

VISION – To be a revolutionary business and create a unique economic opportunity by improving the quality of life for all the citizens we serve.

MISSION – Innovation, Quality, and Value. We at Studio 904 strive to exceed our customers' expectations.

We will accomplish this by:

- Creating an organization committed to lifelong learning.
- Developing a culture that values employees and customers.
- Adhering to business principles of honesty and integrity.
- Responding to the needs of the community and to global changes.
- Providing employment opportunities to a workforce of diverse cultures.

As I stood in front of the mission statement that I developed, I wondered how I would go about exceeding the expectations for people who worked in the nearby art galleries, architectural firms, graphic design firms, and government offices. There was only one way to find out and that was to ask. I grabbed a notebook and a pen and walked down First and Second Avenues between 12:00 p.m. and 1:30 p.m., when the streets were bustling with workers headed to and from lunch. I had never approached total strangers on the street, hoping to strike up a conversation, but this was something I had to do. As the first woman came toward me, I calmed my nerves and walked up to her.

"Hello, my name is Kay. I have a new salon, Studio 904, on the corner of First and Jackson. Would you be willing to answer a few questions for me? I'm trying to get a feel for what the customers in this area want from their salon services," I said.

"Sure, ask me the questions quickly because I only have a limited amount of time before I have to get back to work," she replied.

Her golden hair color looked so appealing and matched the tan sweater and the loose, black pants that ended just above her ankles. Draped down her chest was an artistic, designer necklace that nicely completed the entire outfit. She was the epitome of the modern woman whom, I guessed, worked in the creative design field. It was obvious to me that she and many of the others I talked with, frequently visited upscale downtown salons for their hair services.

I asked the question, "How often do you frequent your hair salon and are you satisfied with what you pay for your hair services?"

A typical response was, "I go in about twice a year to get foil weaves in my hair. I pay $250 and up each time that I go. Plus, there is an additional tipping fee. I'd like to go in to get fresh foil weaves and haircuts every three months, but it's too expensive and doesn't fit into my budget right now."

Two women replied with the same concern: "What puzzles me is that every time I go in for the same service, I get charged different amounts. Oftentimes, I'm presented with a bill at the front desk that is a lot more than I usually pay. When I question the receptionist, she tells me that my stylist added a moisturizing treatment that cost $35. That really bothers me because I should have been told before it was applied to my hair."

Talking to these women gave me valuable information about pricing and customer service. After much thought, I made the following changes in the salon:

- **Clear, up-front pricing for all of our services.** I created a big board in the entryway so clients could see what the charges would be before their services began. There would be no deviation from the listed prices; thus, no surprises for clients when they came to the front desk to pay.

- **In-depth consultations with clients before providing any service.** I insisted that before we touched a hair color brush or brought scissors to a client's hair, we would listen to our clients and agree on the services to be provided. This way, the client would know exactly what would be done and what the total cost would be.

- **Efficient, standardized procedures and teamwork.** To give our customers high-quality results with affordable pricing, we would use the skills of all of our stylists working as a team.

- **No tipping policy.** Giving excellent service would be the norm at our salon. Extra services would not be added on to increase the size of the total bill just so the stylists could receive larger tips.

In order to implement these changes, which were not in line with how the salon industry worked, I knew I had to create and instill a different culture in the salon. *All* of the stylists, and not just a few, had to have excellent technical and communication skills. I would have to harness each of the stylist's skills and have them learn new techniques and work as members of a well-coordinated team. But, how was I going to do that? I knew I had a lot to learn about setting new expectations as well as organizing and operating a business to work like a finely-tuned engine with set time standards and service procedures for everything we did. The biggest question I had was whether my stylists, who were used to working independently for immediate gratification, would want to change and work in this new environment.

While browsing through the Elliott Bay Book Store, which was located across the street from my salon, I ran across a book that piqued my interest. The title of the book was: *"Dr. Deming, The American Who Taught the Japanese About Quality."* I purchased the book and eagerly read it while sitting in the store's coffee shop that was located downstairs. Dr. Deming was sent to Japan after the country was defeated in World War II. Japan was left with very few resources after the war and was desperate to rebuild their economy. At the time, the only items they produced and shipped to other countries were cheaply-made cameras, trinkets, and other small items. I remembered the inexpensive toys I used to play with while living there as a child. After I moved to the United States, I heard numerous American consumers making comments like, "Oh, this is made in Japan. Don't buy it. They aren't made very well and will break easily."

Japan's commerce, however, quickly turned around. In an effort to help the Japanese re-establish their economy, the American government sent Dr. Deming to help them create quality assurance programs in their manufacturing plants. Japan's leaders eagerly learned his philosophy, followed his teachings, and enthusiastically adopted a new way of producing quality products in a more efficient manner. We all know the rest of the story. Automobiles made in Japan soon surpassed the quality of American-made cars. Other products, such as cameras, soon followed. They were able to bring about this transformation by asking customers what they wanted and, in return, producing items efficiently and with good value pricing.

Even after I wore out the pages of Dr. Deming's book, reading every page over and over again, I only had a vague idea about how someone would go about implementing a new philosophy at work and establishing these new quality assurance systems. The question that loomed over me was, "Could we do something like this in our country when the team concept and lifelong learning are not as deeply-rooted in our culture like it is in Japan?" Another question I had was, "How am I going to get the word out to potential customers in the community that Studio 904 was changing the way salon services are provided and they should give us a try?

My husband, Tommy, who was in the silk screen business, knew many of the top graphic design firms in the area. When I shared my concerns about how to best market the salon, he told me about a designer, named Juliette, who worked in the area. "Kay, I think you should meet with Juliette and tell her what you have in mind. I think you will like the simple, holistic designs that she creates."

While meeting with Juliette, I quickly felt that she just might be the designer who could convey the unique attributes about Studio 904 through the use of various marketing pieces.

"Kay, I recommend that we design a simple and tasteful brochure that lists all the unique things about your salon," said Juliette at our first meeting. She brought along a colleague named Bruce. His casual style and demeanor instantly put me at ease. "I brought Bruce with me today because he is a terrific writer. Between my design skills and his writing ability, I'm sure that we can come up with something that translates your philosophy onto a brochure," she explained.

I was surprised when Juliette and Bruce questioned me about what I believed in. No one had ever done that before. The other graphic designers with whom I had worked produced materials from their own points of view and I was never completely happy with the results. The materials never quite conveyed messages that felt like "me."

"Kay, tell me what makes Studio 904 so unique," Juliette asked.

"Well, so many things... I'm not sure I can put them all down into words," I said.

"Don't worry about phrasing them perfectly. Just spill out what's in your gut and we'll take it from there," said Bruce.

For the next hour, they asked what seemed like a hundred questions and I answered each one of them.

After listening intently to how I answered each question, Bruce said, "Kay, you were raised in Japan, right? From the responses that you have given us, it is obvious that you have adopted the "Kaizen" lifestyle in how you live and work. For the last hour, you told us that you believe in continuous improvement so that your employees can grow in their careers and meet or surpass your customers' expectations. You also believe in creating a "win-win" for your business, your employees, your customers, and the community. You don't accept how things are. Instead, you look toward how things can be. You see the BIG picture, not just the world within your salon. All of that translates into what is unique about you. I think we should definitely make "Kaizen" the focus of your promotional materials," said Bruce.

A few weeks later, Juliette came by the salon with a box of beautifully-designed brochures. They were tastefully created with unique folds.

"I hope this meets your expectations," she said, with a smile, as she handed me the large box. "Open it."

I slowly opened the box, holding my breath.

"Oh, these are beautiful, so simple and clean!" I exclaimed.

As I carefully unfolded one of the brochures, the title popped out before my eyes: "KAIZEN: The Art of Lifelong Learning. At Studio 904, we practice the uncommon art of listening and that translates into a style that reflects your personal best."

As Juliette's marketing pieces were distributed throughout the Pioneer Square neighborhood, office workers in nearby buildings gave us a try. At the end of my first year at the new location, I was elated to see my business grow by 40% over the previous year. I'm sure everyone around me thought I was crazy when they saw me jumping up and down screaming, "They love us! We passed their test!"

CHAPTER 17:

I WANT CERTIFIED CLAMS!

Our level of customer service still needed some work to meet my high expectations. I didn't always like the way our clients' haircuts, colors, or styles looked when they left the salon. When I was away from the salon, I worried about what music was playing for our clients. Was the tempo too slow, putting them to sleep, or too upbeat, causing them to be annoyed? Were our clients being listened to or simply being patronized? Did each one get their hair thoroughly shampooed and receive a soothing, scalp massage?

In the middle of the night, I often woke up several times, fretting about clients like Mrs. Tall, whose haircut may have been cut a little too short for her face. I also worried about professional business people, anxiously glancing at their watches while seeing their limited lunch hours disappear as they waited for their appointments. Sometimes, I received scathing customer feedback. Naomi, our front desk coordinator, would often hand me the phone with a worried look on her face. I loved everything about my business, but handling angry customers was always unpleasant.

"Hello, this is Kay speaking. How may I help you, Mrs. Friedman?"

"Kay, I've been coming to your salon for a long time and I've been a loyal customer. You are aware of that, right?

"Yes, I appreciate your patronage very much," I replied.

"I wish you could see what one of your stylists did to my hair color yesterday. It's too red and I have to go to my niece's wedding this weekend. I told her "No red!," but she didn't listen to me. What made me angry was that she didn't seem to care that I was not happy. What are you going to do about this? I'll be the laughing stock of the wedding unless you fix it now!" she screamed in my ear.

"Mrs. Friedman, I'm sorry you are not happy. I understand how upset you are and I will definitely have a talk with the stylist. Rest assured, I promise you that I will personally make it right," I replied. My heart thumped so hard, I felt like it was going to jump out of my body.

"I don't have much time. I need to get it fixed today," she replied.

"I'll do anything. I will stay this evening to re-color your hair. Please come in and let me do that for you," I pleaded. My mouth felt dry and my throat was closing up. Thankfully, she accepted my offer. I didn't want to lose any clients at the salon, let alone one of my best ones.

When these unfortunate incidents happened, I struggled with what to say to my employees. They typically insisted that the customers were wrong or that it wasn't fair for me to always side with the customer. I didn't want to become the type of boss that employees dreaded seeing every day when they came to work. More importantly, I wanted to maintain a consistently happy workplace.

Every stylist I hired had a unique personality and skill set, but I wasn't sure that all of them understood how to make people look and feel not only good, but great. I didn't know how to correct them without creating hard feelings. Even though I knew the questions, I didn't always have the answers. How could I create a salon where all the customers walked out happy because they got what they wanted and more? How could I get every stylist to care about their clients and take pride in their work?

On a cold February morning, I was driving along First Avenue in downtown Seattle to attend a meeting. As I entered the waterfront district, I noticed a huge, colorful billboard on the side of the road with a picture of gigantic, shiny clams. The sign proclaimed "We are Ivar's, Seattle's Famous Seafood Restaurant. Our clams are better because WE SERVE CERTIFIED CLAMS!"

That's it! I remember saying out loud to myself in the car, "I want certified employees! No... not just certified employees... I want SKILLED AND CERTIFIED employees!"

After this "aha" moment, I decided to write a procedural handbook to outline what it meant to be a "skilled and certified employee" in my salon. For more than two years, I worked on my manual every day. I wrote step-by-step procedures on how to perform every service we offered to our customers in the salon. It included topics such as "How to give a great shampoo," "How to listen to our customers' wants and needs," and "The procedures for a great haircut, color, and perm." I included everything I knew about personal and professional development, such as how to use positive words when communicating with customers and team members. I established a salon dress code policy, and listed the responsibilities of being a good citizen. I painstakingly developed a "skills certification test" and a scoring system for each service we offered in the salon.

While writing, I drew a lot of inspiration from my Japanese heritage. Consistent with my new marketing theme, I decided to call it *The Book of Kaizen*, based on the well-known philosophy of lifelong learning that I was trying to implement not only in my work, but also in my personal life. I introduced the book to my staff and held weekly training sessions with them. The skills certification tests became very important to the stylists. After all, pay increases were given to those who passed the tests and demonstrated a higher skill level in their work.

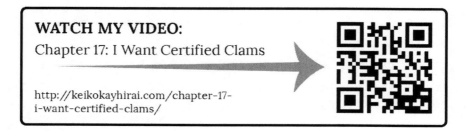

WATCH MY VIDEO:
Chapter 17: I Want Certified Clams

http://keikokayhirai.com/chapter-17-i-want-certified-clams/

Over time, I became the happy and proud owner of a business that improved dramatically over a fairly short period of time. The staff and I started with little knowledge or mutual understanding of our core business values and principles. Quickly, however, we established a culture of continuous learning and growth. It was amazing to see everyone's confidence increase. Equally important was watching our customers walk out of the salon with smiles on their faces. I couldn't imagine a better feeling.

The *Book of Kaizen* remains a work in progress. These days, I rarely tap a stylist on the shoulder to say, "You are not doing it right." Instead, I say things like "Jenny, I love how you gave that great shampoo! Your customer had the biggest grin on her face while you were shampooing her hair. I even heard her say, "Ah, that felt so-o-o good!" when she got up from the shampoo chair."

When I showed the *Book of Kaizen* to a colleague, she was amazed that it was so comprehensive. "Kay, this is great! It doesn't surprise me that you put in the effort to include step-by-step procedures for all of Studio 904's services. This book will certainly help all of your stylists to provide the quality services that you have been working so hard to provide to all of your customers. I give you an A+!"

CHAPTER 18:

WHEN THE GOVERNOR

COMES CALLING

In the midst of an early morning rush in the salon one day, I was called to the front desk. "Kay, there's a phone call for you," said Naomi, our front desk manager. "I'm busy right now and can't take the time to talk on the phone," I called out. Naomi said, "I think you'd better take this call. The governor's office in Olympia is on the phone." My first thought was, "Oh no. What did I do? Was my sales tax payment late? Did I forget to mail my check to the Washington State Department of Labor and Industries?"

I ran to the phone, quickly picked up the receiver, and said, "Hello, this is Kay. How may I help you?"

"Hello Kay, this is Robin Pollard from Governor Mike Lowry's office. Your name was recommended to us by a number of people. The Governor would like to extend an invitation to you to become a member of "The Governor's Small Business Improvement Council." This group does just as the name indicates; it works to improve the business climate for small businesses in our state," she said.

I was dumbfounded, but pulled myself together to say, "Oh, I think I have to decline. I am the least political person around."

"You are underestimating yourself. Your name was referred to us from the mayor's office in Seattle. You received the "Mayor's Small Business Award" four months ago, correct? We have received glowing reports about you and have heard that you are a true leader and advocate for small businesses."

"I wish. I'm only a struggling small business owner," I replied.

"Would you be able to join us in two weeks for our April meeting in Olympia?" Robin asked.

"I'm not sure," I said hesitating.

"Why don't you consider a one-time visit to see if it appeals to you?" she asked.

Because I didn't have the guts to say "no" to this representative from the governor's office, I cautiously agreed. After I hung up, I wondered what I was getting myself into. How do I get to the state capitol in Olympia? I'd never been there before.

The Governor's Small Business Improvement Council was comprised of small business owners from all corners of the state and the heads of state agencies whose policies affected small businesses. We met once a month to discuss, debate, and make recommendations to the Governor on matters that impacted the well-being of small businesses in Washington. The first few meetings were intimidating and grueling. I wasn't familiar with all of the government acronyms and abbreviations, so it was hard for me to understand everything that was discussed. In addition, I knew very little about the legislative process in our state. Once I began to understand the complex maze of how the state and federal government systems worked, I was able to contribute to the discussions and make my opinions heard. It flattered me when people would occasionally say, "Are you sure you are a hairstylist? You missed your calling! You should think about running for public office."

I soon realized what a privilege it was to be included in this group of entrepreneurs. We had access to important information and the opportunity to influence state policies related to small businesses. When I met other business owners in the community, they curiously asked, "What do you do when you serve on the Governor's Council? You must not be doing much! The business and occupation tax I pay on my business still hasn't gone down a penny; every year, it keeps going up!" I answered, "If you only knew the kinds of things that the government is doing to protect your business. You would be shocked at the number of proposed policies discussed that, if adopted, could negatively impact small businesses. Fortunately, the Governor listens to the Council's recommendations and they rarely see the light of day." I didn't mention all the last-minute trips that I made to Olympia in the early morning hours to explain to legislative committee members how a particular bill would impose undue hardships on small businesses in the state.

After participating for two years on the Council, I was appointed Chairperson of the Governor's Small Business Improvement Council and was selected as one of five delegates to represent Washington State at the National Small Business Conference in Washington, D.C. The first day, we met briefly with President Bill Clinton and Vice-President Al Gore and then worked for five solid days with their respective staff members. Our task was to develop a comprehensive plan to improve the U.S. economy by amending federal regulations for small businesses. I regret that one of the things we were unable to do was to create a friendlier environment within the Internal Revenue Service. To this day, most small business owners are intimidated by the IRS with their strict regulations and enforcement procedures. Two weeks after returning from Washington, D.C., Vice-President Gore sent a letter informing the conference delegates that two of our recommendations were already being implemented. I was happy to know that my time and energy in D.C. was well-spent.

That same summer, Governor Lowry summoned the members of the Small Business Improvement Council to a special meeting. The notice read, "I'd like to invite the Council to discuss a critical issue: "Workforce Training in Our State."

The drive to Olympia was almost an hour, but I didn't mind. As chairperson of the Council, I always looked forward to doing whatever I could to improve the conditions for small businesses in our state. When I climbed the steps to enter our state's capitol building, I felt a surge of excitement when I thought about the prospect of helping the Governor of the state of Washington solve a critical and time-sensitive issue.

The governor's conference room, located adjacent to his office on the second floor of the capitol building, was large and stately. The intricately-designed, upholstered chairs surrounded a large, rectangular, mahogany table. The council members sat poised around the table. After salutations, everyone settled in and thumbed through the twenty-page report that was presented to each member.

Quietly, the door opened. In came a member of the governor's staff. The whole room became instantly silent. "Good morning council members. Thank you for coming on such short notice. The Governor will be arriving shortly," she said, as she sat down next to the governor's chair.

A few minutes later, the door opened and in came Governor Lowry. He had a stocky build and was wearing a dark suit with a paisley-printed necktie. His wavy hair was salt-and-pepper in color and his round and jovial face looked more like a friendly uncle than a politician. We were instantly put at ease with his affable and casual mannerisms. After making a short, welcome speech, he began telling us in detail what he had on his mind. "I have a big concern. Microsoft has built a university in Beijing, China. They are recruiting and training young Chinese students from the ground level up to learn their best business practices. When the students graduate, they will be recruited to Microsoft's Redmond campus, just outside of Seattle, to work," he explained, as he looked at us intently. We sat silently waiting for his next words. "What do you think this will do to the workforce in our state?" he asked.

The Governor continued while we listened in silence.

"Do you know how many people we have in our state who are eager to work but remain unemployed or under-employed because they don't have the necessary skills? This population is made up largely of single mothers, high school drop-outs, and a fast-growing number of immigrants who don't speak the English language. They are on welfare and live off of our state funds - our tax dollars. Using his well-known gesture of waving both hands in the air emphatically, the Governor exclaimed, "It is absolutely essential for us to find a way to get our population trained and working!" He continued, "And I don't mean low-paid, no-growth jobs either. Most of these workers will be hired by small businesses. They are your future workforce. Businesses and schools must work together to ensure that we have a foundation of well-trained employees. It is the only way to keep your businesses open in the coming years."

I raised my hand and asked, "Governor Lowry, you are saying that there is a large pool of people who are desperate to work. I've been putting want ads for hair stylists in the newspapers on a regular basis for weeks and haven't had any success. No one applies for these jobs, so where are the people who want to work?" The Governor answered, "Kay, people don't apply for jobs like yours because they don't have the skills to be productive in your business. Before you can put them to work, you need to train them."

Michael, a hardware store owner from Yakima said, "But how will we be able to do that? We're not the Boeing Company. We lack the resources to implement a big, sophisticated, training program. Our cash flow is so tight that we can't even pay ourselves some weeks." The Governor responded, "I hear you, Michael. Business is tough. But, we must find a way. Moving trucks are rolling into our state every day, bringing employees from other states and from overseas, while our own people live in poverty and remain unemployed. Businesses will close their doors, not because there are no customers, but because they won't have the employees to serve their customers. This scenario is not a healthy one and we will all be doomed unless we figure out a way to turn this around."

Governor Lowry assigned us the responsibility of putting together a six-member task force to come up with innovative ideas for a workforce training program that could be implemented in our state. The task force had a deadline of four months to finish the project and turn in their recommendations. Of course, I was excited at the challenge and immediately signed up to be a member.

First, the task force contacted community colleges, high schools, the Washington State Employment Security Department, trade unions, and large companies to learn about their training programs. One of those large companies, the Boeing Company, shared their nationally-recognized training program with us. We also brought in experts who taught us how European apprenticeship models worked. Their "learn as you earn" programs had a high success rate in helping non-college-bound students obtain jobs that promised advancement in their chosen career paths. In addition, we interviewed personnel from different industry sectors (e.g., electricians and plumbers) and asked about the skills that were necessary for individuals to enter those trades. Our partnership with community colleges included writing a "skill standards" book for four different industries. I was elated that cosmetology was chosen as one of those industries. Working with a team of eight salon owners who I had recruited, we identified the skills that stylists needed to be successful in the industry.

In my spare time, I walked around the campuses of several community colleges in our state. I was surprised to see so many foreign students, especially women of color. From previous experiences, I knew that foreign students who attended college in the United States often displayed a good work ethic and were eager to learn. I quickly sensed that some of these students might be my future stylists.

Because of my standing as a member of the Governor's Task Force for Workforce Training, I had access to community college instructors who were open to answering a number of pointed questions: "Where are your students from? What are they learning? Where will they go to work after they graduate? What challenges do they have? What will it take to help them succeed in the workplace?" The answers I received were exactly what I suspected. The instructors taught the students but many had no idea what their students would be doing or where they would be going to work once they graduated and left the campus.

The members of the task force worked furiously for four months and submitted a comprehensive "Washington State Workforce Training Plan" to the governor's office. On the first page of this document, just inside the front cover, we stated in bold letters: **"Dedicated to Our Future Workforce... Immigrant Women, Single-Mothers, At-Risk High-School Students, and People on Welfare..."**

What I learned while serving on this task force was invaluable to me personally, as well as to my business. I stopped recruiting experienced stylists, many of whom disliked taking directions or learning new methods. Instead, I searched for the under-served populations of people who were eager to learn new skills and build a career.

I am glad that I took the initial call from the governor's office. It was a joy to work with the Governor. Unlike most elected officials, his demeanor was never pompous or intimidating. When I talked with him, he made me feel like I was speaking to a next-door neighbor and seemed sincerely interested in our discussions. During one luncheon that he hosted for the committee members, he asked, "Kay, how is your haircutting business doing?" I replied, "Governor Lowry, we don't just cut people's hair, we make people feel good about themselves by bringing out their personal best." He laughed and said, "See, this is how much I know about what you do." From that day on, he never failed to ask, "Kay, I know that you are still probably focused on raising the self-esteem of each one of your customers. How many customers did you help today?"

Aside from being a down-to-earth, "good guy," Governor Lowry was a strong advocate for small businesses. With his steadfast support, the Council initiated programs that are still helping businesses today. Our Task Force on Workforce Training inspired me to implement the recommendations we made to the Governor in my salon.

CHAPTER 19:

THE RAIN IN SPAIN FALLS MAINLY
IN THE PLAINS

Determined to "walk the talk" after my positive experiences with state and federal government, I was enthusiastic about taking what I had learned to start making a difference in my own community. My experiences taught me the importance of having one's ideas and opinions heard in the right places – when you articulate your ideas, philosophy, and vision, people begin to appreciate what you stand for. Because of the number of times that I testified at legislative forums, the Washington State Workforce Training boards, and with community college committees, my name became synonymous with employment and training programs within the government and education sectors in our state. Soon, I began receiving numerous phone calls from counselors and educators who wanted me to speak about on-the-job training. I even spoke at health care organizations and trained their nurses and technicians on how to improve customer service.

I also received numerous calls from job coaches and counselors with clients who were interested in working in the cosmetology industry. Most of the phone requests went something like this: "Kay, I am trying to help a young mother from Ecuador who is interested in working at a hair salon that offers some kind of on-the-job training. I've heard so much about your job training program, so I would like to bring her to your salon and see if you would be interested in hiring her. Would you be amenable to meeting with us?" I didn't have the heart to turn anyone down. Instead, I took the time to meet with potential employees and provide an assessment of what they needed to learn before they were ready to work in a salon like mine. I hired several individuals who were recent immigrants to this country, but as time went on, there were more applicants than I was able to employ.

"Are there other salons like Studio 904 who are willing to train their new hires and pay them an hourly wage?" a counselor asked.

"Unfortunately, this industry's practices are chair-rental or commission-based and new entrants are required to build their own clientele," I explained.

"Then how can stylists possibly learn the skills of the trade?" she asked.

I responded, "If they work in a commission-based salon, each stylist must first become an apprentice to one of the senior stylists in the salon. As an apprentice, you are typically assigned to do all of the shampoos, clean hair brushes and combs, sweep up after the senior stylists, and any other work that is assigned by the owner to help the salon run smoothly. When I started out in the industry, I remember running out every day to pick up lunches for the senior stylists."

"So, how did you learn your cutting and coloring skills?" a job coach inquired.

"I pretty much learned by observing the senior stylists when I wasn't busy, I replied. "In return for my menial services, I was told that a senior stylist would train me after the salon closed for the day. Occasionally, I received some training, but not always. Oftentimes, they were too tired to teach me after standing and cutting hair for eight hours."

Another counselor asked, "How long did you have to work as an apprentice?"

"For about a year, after I graduated from cosmetology school," I responded. "After that, the owner of the salon assigned me a chair and told me to find my own paying clients. I struggled for many years and tried to make a decent commission based on the few clients that I was able to work with on a regular basis."

The counselor looked discouraged. "I know the students we are trying to place would never make it on a commission or chair rental system," she said. "I studied the recent industry statistics and found that 80% of students graduating from cosmetology programs leave the industry within two years. In our case, the rate would probably be around 100% with the students we have."

I hired Lan after she graduated from a cosmetology program at a local community college. She was a young woman from Viet Nam and I was excited to hire my first immigrant stylist who had no formal, on-the-job training. On her first day at work, Lan came into the salon an hour before her scheduled time to learn English in the back room of the salon.

"Good morning, Lan, are you ready to start our class?" I said, with a smile on my face as she came running in the door.

"Good morning, Ma'am," she greeted me, trying to catch her breath.

"Looks like you have already had a busy morning, Lan," I said.

"Yes, Ma'am. I took my two children to their pre-school. The bus was late and I missed the next bus that I usually take to come downtown," Lan said.

"You mean you take your kids to school on a bus and then you transfer to another bus to come to work?" I asked.

"Yes, Ma'am.

I looked at her in disbelief. She had been up since 5:00 a.m., juggling the needs of her children and dealing with the sometimes unreliable, public transportation system. I couldn't help but admire her strength and commitment to building a life for herself and her children in a new country. "Lan, let's begin our class. You will be speaking English and cutting and styling your clients' hair in no time," I promised.

Two weeks later, after practicing her cutting and styling skills on mannequins and learning some rudimentary English, I scheduled her first haircut with a client named Ken. Standing behind one of the doorways, anxiously peeking out at our design floor, I was relieved to see that Lan was executing a perfect haircut for Ken. She neatly combed each section of his hair, held his hair up at the right angle, and slid her scissors through to cut, just the way I had taught her. I thought to myself, this is the best haircut and style I have seen on Ken. Relieved, I walked into my office to make a quick phone call.

Suddenly, I heard a commotion at the front desk and ran to see what was happening. When I arrived, Ken was in the process of paying for his haircut. When he saw me, he immediately waved his credit card in the air and yelled, "Kay, what the hell are you trying to do here? You're turning Studio 904 into a training center!" He startled me, but I got the nerve to ask him, "Ken, is there something wrong with your haircut?" "No, it isn't the haircut," he scowled. "That stylist you gave me can't even speak English. I'm paying a lot of money for my haircut, so I expect a stylist who speaks English to cut my hair. Where is Jen, who usually cuts my hair?" he demanded.

I wanted to tell him the truth, but I decided to keep quiet and hear him out. What I didn't tell him is that I had to let Jen go because I couldn't keep a stylist who treated our customers and her team members so poorly. I also wanted to tell him that Jen didn't really care about making sure he was happy with his haircut. Her main concern was to get her work done as quickly as possible so that she could sit in the back room, talk on her phone, or read the latest gossip magazines.

Instead, I kept my composure. Using my well-practiced, soothing voice, I said, "Ken, I want you to know that every decision I make for my salon is based on keeping my customers happy. Lan gave you a really flattering haircut. She is trying very hard to learn English, in addition to learning new technical skills." Ken stood there in silence and glared at me. "Did you know that I was like Lan twenty years ago?" I asked. "I was intimidated and scared because I couldn't speak a word of English after my mother brought me here from Japan when I was eleven years old. I'm certain that your behavior scared Lan. If you are not willing to give Lan the support she needs to build a better life here, I don't think I want you as a client."

"Well, fine. I'm never coming back," he shouted. Ken angrily stomped out of the salon and slammed the door as he exited. My whole body was shaking. I had never "fired" a customer before. I asked myself, "What did I just do? Am I crazy?"

Thinking about the incident with Ken left me deep in thought that afternoon. I began to doubt myself and my intentions and thought that maybe it was unreasonable to think that I could train a group of immigrants to succeed in the cosmetology industry. Could the majority of my clients really be so intolerant that they would only accept English-speaking stylists? Was this the beginning of the end of Studio 904?

The next morning, while I was giving Lan a training class on how to handle angry customers, I received a call from Ken. My heart started to beat quickly because I assumed he was calling to repeat yesterday's angry words. "Good morning, Ken, how may I help you?" I said, trying to sound upbeat. There was a short period of silence. "Kay, I want to apologize for my behavior yesterday. I came home and thought about what I had said and done to you and Lan and I felt terrible. I even called myself "a jerk," he said meekly. "No problem Ken, I'm happy that you are seeing things differently today," I said, cheerfully. Ken responded, "I want you to know that I support how you are training your staff members and I can hardly wait to see what Lan will be like in a year. Thank you for doing this." "Oh, Ken, thank you for this good news!" I replied. Needless to say, I was walking on cloud nine for the rest of the day. My faith in the true goodness of the human spirit had been restored.

Next came a stylist named Hanh. She was referred to me by Ms. Hayes, a cosmetology instructor. "Kay, I hope that you will hire Hanh and train her in the same way that you have been teaching some of our other students. She is talented, but lacks self-confidence because she does not have a good grasp of English. I want her to have the same excellent training that you are so well-known for in the community."

When Hanh came in for an assessment of her technical skills, I was taken aback by how gracefully her hands and fingers moved while cutting her model's hair. "She is a diamond in the rough!" I thought to myself. I hired her immediately and began her training. After I watched Hanh work with customers, I noticed that her social interactions were awkward and could be viewed, by some, as inappropriate in a business setting.

"Hanh, customers in our country don't understand why you giggle and look away when they thank you for the beautiful hair style that you have given them," I said. Hanh gave me a puzzled look, but said nothing. "In your country, giggling may be acceptable, but here in the United States, it can come across as insulting," I explained.

"What should I be doing?" Hanh asked.

"When customers praise you for your good work, just look them in the eyes and say, "Thank you. I think this style is flattering to your face. I'm glad that you like it, I said. Hanh repeated the phrase after me but her heavy accent made it hard to understand. How could I explain this to Hanh, who had so much talent? After a sleepless night, I came up with a solution that I thought might work.

The next morning, I went to work with a VHS tape of "My Fair Lady." Featuring Audrey Hepburn, it was one of my favorite movies. When Hanh came in that morning, I could hardly wait to give it to her. "Hanh, I think I have the perfect training program for you. This tape is a movie called "My Fair Lady." The main actress is a famous movie star named Audrey Hepburn. When you watch this tape, you will see how Professor Higgins teaches Eliza Doolittle how to improve her speech and speak her words with perfect pronunciation. I will play the tape now so we can watch it together.

After the movie ended, I could see that Hanh was deep in thought. "I'd like to practice the way Eliza Doolittle did it in the movie... THE RAIN IN SPAIN STAYS MAINLY IN THE PLAINS," she said, with a big smile on her face. I made up a big poster board with that well-known phrase written in bold, black letters. Every day, for the next month, Hanh and I practiced saying the phrase to each other: "THE... RAIN... IN... SPAIN... STAYS... MAINLY... IN... THE... PLAINS."

Hanh's articulation of this phrase slowly improved as she repeated it over and over. In three weeks, her overall speaking ability improved and she was much easier to understand. The story of Eliza Doolittle's transformation from a street urchin into a beautiful, gracious lady gave Hanh the confidence that she could break out from her self-imposed shell if she practiced as hard as Eliza Doolittle did. I was so proud of her when she stopped giggling, looked her clients in the eyes, and responded appropriately to their compliments, "Thank you. I think this cut and style looks very nice on you." It was too bad that Audrey Hepburn would never know how her infamous catch-phrase had helped Hanh, and possibly other immigrant women, gain their self-confidence.

One day, I received an offer from the City of Seattle's Youth Employment Department to teach a series of classes to students on the necessary skills to get a job. They agreed to fund the staff time that it would take to develop and deliver this training program.

Together, with Tassie Christopher, a human resources consultant, I used some of the materials we had in our in-house training book to develop a training program. We trained two of the stylists at Studio 904 to be on our teaching team, which turned out to be a good move on our part. The stylists we chose came from backgrounds that were very similar to the lives of the students in the class, making it easy for them to relate to these students' experiences. We put together a two-week class and titled it "Branding Your Uniqueness." The six modules of the training program consisted of information to help students build a healthy self-esteem through communication, goal setting, and follow-through skills. A large portion of the training was dedicated to dressing appropriately at school and using appropriate language and gestures when interacting with other students and teachers.

The first day of class was a little nerve-wracking. Tassie and I, together with our "rookie teachers," stood in front of twenty-four students between the ages of 15 and 18 years. These students were chosen for this class because they were labeled as "at risk" students by the school. "These students have no direction and they are lost," explained one of the counselors. I replied, "I hope that we will be able to help them. We designed a lot of short, interactive training segments that are combined with small "giveaways," like comics and movie passes, to keep their attention and encourage participation." By the second session, the students and teaching team were beginning to feel comfortable with each other. The room was filled with laughter and cooperation. I wondered how these fun-loving kids could be labeled as being so lost in school. They seemed joyful and enthused. What was also heartwarming to me was to see my stylists developing their teaching and communication skills at the same time.

When we had a moment during one of the breaks, Tassie pulled me aside and said, "Kay, do you realize that this class is creating a "win-win" situation for us? We are not only teaching these students some lifelong skills, but your employees are also stepping up their skills as well." "Yes, this is exactly what I was trying to tell the naysayers when they claimed that small businesses wouldn't be able to train our young people to be productive members of the community. I was repeatedly told that the only thing that small businesses would be able to offer would be low-wage, no-growth jobs," I said. "Well, you are definitely proving them wrong," she said, with a big grin on her face. Tassie's own personal accomplishments were so admirable that hearing these sincere words of approval from her meant the world to me.

When the fourth class in the series rolled around, Jonathan's seat was empty. I was puzzled because he had had perfect attendance up to this point. In fact, he usually showed up fifteen minutes early because he enjoyed helping us prepare for the class by passing out study materials. I asked the program's counselor if she knew where he was. She said that she had not heard from him that morning.

At 10:30 a.m., the door slowly opened and Jonathan came walking in, looking somewhat embarrassed. He quietly walked to his desk and sat down. I looked at him, but he looked away. After catching his attention, I motioned for him to step out into the hallway with me.

"Jonathan, you made a personal commitment to show up to these eight sessions on time so that you would finish with a perfect attendance record."

He looked down at the floor and answered, "Yes Ma'am."

"So why did you break your promise, Jonathan?" I probed.

He stood in silence.

"Please give me an explanation. Otherwise, I will have to report your absence to the program manager," I explained.

"Well, we had an incident at my house early this morning," he mumbled.

I asked, "What kind of an incident, Jonathan?"

"My mom's ex-boyfriend broke into our house and started beating her up."

Incredulous, I asked, "What? Are you telling me the truth?"

"I heard her screams from my upstairs bedroom so I ran downstairs, he replied. This dude had a gun in his hand so I ran out of our house to the next-door neighbor's house, and started pounding on their door. When the neighbor guy came to the door, I told him to call 911."

"Oh, my gosh! That's terrible!" I gasped, in disbelief.

"The police arrived shortly and went into my house, Jonathan explained. "They arrested my mom's ex-boyfriend and hauled him off to jail. He was high on cocaine and didn't know what he was doing."

"So what did you do next?" I asked.

"It took me a while to straighten up the house and calm my mom down," he said.

"And after going through all this, you still got ready and took the bus to get here, even though you knew you were going to be late?" I asked.

"Yes, Ma'am," Jonathan whispered.

After hearing his story, I felt like I was the one with the problem. I was ashamed that I had not taken the time to understand and appreciate the often difficult environments and the issues faced by many "at risk" students. Jonathan was in a "no win" situation. He lived in a world that he did not ask to be born into. I gave him a long hug and told him, "Jonathan, you are a hero!" I admired him for making the effort to show up to class after all he had gone through that morning.

Everyone knows that life is not always fair. I constantly remind myself that it takes a compassionate village to raise our children. And, after my experience with Jonathan and others like him, I committed myself to participate in efforts to improve the lives of children on an ongoing basis.

CHAPTER 20:

WORK ON MY BUSINESS,
NOT IN MY BUSINESS

Startled by the sudden ringing of the office phone late one evening, I woke up and quickly ran to answer it without fully realizing what was going on. I had apparently dozed off because there were creases on my cheek where I had fallen asleep on top of a pile of paperwork.

"Yes? Tommy?" I muttered, half-heartedly into the phone receiver.

"Why are you still at the salon? It's almost midnight!" my husband exclaimed, without so much as a hello.

"Oh, sorry. I had so much to catch up on in the office," I apologized.

"I already fed, bathed, and put the kids to bed," Tommy said.

"Thank you. I'll be home in a little while," I assured him.

"I'm worried about you. I don't want you to drive yourself into the ground over your business. It's not worth it," he replied, with an air of concern.

"I promise, I won't," as I tiredly placed the receiver back on the phone.

Don't let anyone tell you otherwise. Running a small business is far from glamorous. On most days, I was the first one to work and the last one to leave. I felt like I promised my husband a hundred times that I would be home early and would not work so hard. Every day involved checking voicemails, scheduling client appointments, making coffee, and cleaning the restroom at regular intervals. In addition, each morning, I conducted a "quality circle" with my staff to make sure we were all on the same page about what we wanted to accomplish that day. This brief get-together was an effort to ensure that we could all start the day feeling positive about ourselves and our work.

The hours flew by in the salon. From the time the salon opened in the morning, until early evening, I served clients one after another in what became a blur of faces and hair. On most days, I only had time to run into the back room to take two bites out of my sandwich and a sip of water before running back onto the floor.

Most of the stylists that worked for me were not as busy. I couldn't help but resent their down time, while I was constantly busy with back-to-back appointments. It was like watching payroll dollars slowly trickle down the drain. To make matters worse and to highlight my own dilemma, I received a phone call one afternoon from a friend named Rana. She was an old high school classmate who owned a popular organic restaurant in the city. It served delicious comfort food and was always full of customers.

"Kay, I want to break the news to you before you hear it from someone else," my friend said hesitantly. "I'm closing my restaurant in two weeks."

"What? You must be kidding! Why?" I exclaimed.

"I am so burned out," she said. "I have no life because I am working twelve hours a day, seven days a week."

"Just like me," I replied, as I commiserated with her.

"Have you ever figured out how much you're making per hour? she asked.

I meekly replied, "No, I'm kind of afraid to know the answer."

"Well, I did, and I'm making around $4.50 per hour! It can't possibly be worth it, she said. These long hours are killing me. I need to come to my senses and quit before I get really sick."

"I hate to see you make a rash decision," I tried to tell her. "Hang in there, Rana, things will get better!"

"Nope, I'm done," she said firmly. "I wish you the best of luck with your business. But you should remember... $4.50 an hour."

I hung up and felt my eyes burn. Feeling like a lone wolf, I wondered to myself whether I was the last one standing in this seemingly impossible race to succeed as a small business owner.

Shortly after my conversation with Rana, I asked Naomi, my loyal front desk coordinator, "What can we do so that the other stylists are busier than they are now?"

"Unfortunately, as it stands now, the majority of our clients want you and *only you*," she said.

"I can't be a one-woman circus forever!" I complained. "There is no time to train anyone, I'm almost burnt out like my friend, and I'll be divorced soon if I can't come up with a way to spread the load to some of the other stylists."

Thankfully, Naomi was unfazed by my grouchiness. Instead, she quickly pulled out a newsletter from the Seattle Chamber of Commerce. In one of the columns on the front page, there was an announcement that read: "We invite you to attend a live lecture by Michael E. Gerber, author of *The E-Myth - Why Most Small Businesses Don't Work and What to Do About It*." In my current mood, I had to attend.

The workshop was held in the Chamber's downtown office and began with the usual complimentary coffee, muffins, and polite exchange of pleasantries. After about a half-hour, Michael Gerber walked to the front of the room, cleared his throat, and said something that definitely struck a chord with me:

"I know all of you sitting in this room started your own business because you are good technicians and you love to do whatever you are doing. But, I bet you came to this workshop because you're exhausted, in debt, and wondering what to do next. What you need to know, and what I'm here to teach you, is that there *is* a difference between technicians, managers, and entrepreneurs. As far as I'm concerned, if you want your business to succeed in the long run, you *must* become a true entrepreneur."

He held up his best-selling book, *E-Myth*, and thumbed through the pages gingerly as he said, "I named my book, *E-Myth*, because people who own a small business often have big misconceptions about being entrepreneurs. I'm here to teach you the myth about business ownership and how to turn yourself around from being a technician in your struggling business to an owner of a 'turnkey' business - a business that is ready for immediate operation."

"The benefit of becoming an entrepreneur is that you will stay passionate and love what you do in your business not only today, but also fifty years from now, he continued. "It will give you continuous opportunities to learn and help you grow into a person who is alive and happy until your last day on this earth."

"Here's the secret: If you want to become an entrepreneur, you must learn to work *on* your business, not *in* your business."

When I heard that, my eyes must have been as wide as saucers. I finally felt like someone understood the source of most of my problems.

Mr. Gerber pointed to me.

"Kay, what kind of business do you own?"

"A hair salon," I replied.

"You opened the salon because you have the technical ability to cut, color, and style hair, right? And you think you can do it better than anyone else around, right?"

I was a bit embarrassed, but everything he was saying was true, I thought to myself.

He looked around the room. "All of you... If you are a dentist, a plumber, an engineer, or a musician, you believe that by understanding the technical work of the business, you're qualified to run a business that does that kind of work, right?" he asked.

We all nodded in agreement.

"It's simply *not* true!" he responded. "In fact, rather than being your single greatest asset, knowing the technical side of your business is your greatest liability!"

I found myself involuntarily grinning with joy. Gerber explained one business concept after another. Despite his initial, rather formal demeanor, he eventually turned out to be a very warm and friendly person. He gave me total confidence that he knew his subject inside and out. One of the most frightening facts he pointed out was that, historically, small businesses fail after three or less years. Some of the other information he shared was more encouraging, though, and he convinced me that I possessed the tools to beat those odds.

That evening, I stayed up most of the night reading his book. I could barely force myself to sleep for a few hours before jumping up to write a plan for my business. By incorporating his ideas with my own, I could update and enhance my handbook to include all of the information that was necessary to improve the skills of my stylists. Suddenly, my mind was racing a hundred miles an hour! Based on Mr. Gerber's presentation, I decided to use his words for my plan: "WORK ON MY BUSINESS, NOT IN MY BUSINESS." Here are some of the key points I wrote down:

Look at my business from the outside in, not from the inside out.

Write out a procedure for every service the salon provides.

Teach the procedures to the stylists.

Hire people and train them to do things better than I can.

Don't hire experts. Hire new people with positive attitudes who want to learn, and teach them what they need to know.

Spend my time doing the right things to improve my business, so that my business will take on its own life.

The first step I had to take was to reduce the amount of time that I spent cutting hair. I immediately reduced the time that I had with my clients in half and used the time to teach my employees so that they could provide the same level of services that I had been doing. All went well until the middle of February. February was always a slow month, but on this particular day, the salon was completely empty.

Deeply concerned, I asked Naomi, "Where are all of the customers?"

"I had some calls, but your clients refused to have their hair styled by anyone but you," she explained.

"Did you tell them that I'm training our stylists to cut and color hair just like I do?" I asked.

"Yes, I told that to everyone," she replied.

"Did you tell them that I trained them to be better than me?" I probed.

"Yes, I told them but they said they don't believe that. They still want you to do their hair."

Still anxious, I asked Naomi, "Have all of the promotional mailers been sent out?"

"I sent everything out a week ago," she confirmed.

A bit dazed, I bit my lip and fell silent. I had done everything the way I planned, but I couldn't afford to wait much longer for results. Payroll was due soon and there were not enough clients on the immediate horizon to bring in the needed revenue. I knew that one of my choices was a non-starter; I couldn't pick up my sheers and start seeing all my clients again because I would be returning to the same exhausting merry-go-round I was trying to get off. Determined to stick to my plan, I decided to keep working hard to drive my knowledge into the heads and hands of my employees.

My solution was to create a training program named, "The Customer Trainer." Here's how it worked: I invited my clients to get their hair cut, styled, or colored by me while one of the salon's stylists stood by and observed my consultation and haircutting techniques. Then, I invited the customer to come back for a complimentary service with the same stylist who had previously observed me; this time around, I supervised the stylist. During this supervised session, I encouraged the customer to give their honest feedback by saying, for example, "Yes, I like that or I'd like that a little fuller on top."

The important lesson I learned from implementing my program is that clients loved being part of the evaluation process because it gave them a voice on how they wanted their hair done; they also loved being a teacher and mentor to our stylists. For the stylists, it reinforced the importance of listening closely to their clients. I decided this training program was a thousand times more effective than using plastic mannequins with implanted artificial hair. Mannequins could never provide the human feedback that is so important to improving and growing, no matter what the field or profession. I added this teaching experience to my *Book of Kaizen* along with the following reminder: "Customers are our best trainers. At Studio 904, we work WITH our customers, not ON them."

Training my stylists and showing clients that my team could produce pleasing results, took hours of my time and months of implementation. When I became exhausted and discouraged, I repeated the E-Myth mantra I learned from Michael Gerber, "WORK ON YOUR BUSINESS, NOT IN YOUR BUSINESS."

Months later, my time and efforts were rewarded. Most of my clients who participated in the Customer Training program agreed to have their hair done by one of the other stylists instead of me. What won them over is that they realized the obvious benefits of flexible scheduling when someone other than myself could take care of their hair care needs just as well as I could. With the success of the program, the workload became more evenly distributed with everyone in the salon pulling their weight and contributing to the success of the salon. Pleasantly reassured, I realized that I was now steadfast in my goal to become an entrepreneur instead of a technician.

In today's environment, I enjoy working with a team of professional stylists, who have all been trained by me, and trained to be better than me, in every service that Studio 904 offers. After years of hard work and a lot of frustration, I finally achieved my goal of becoming a socially conscious entrepreneur who strives to do good things for the community in which I work. At the same time, I am able to expand my learning while sustaining my passion for work and making our customers happy. In the process, I have created a sustainable business that runs like clockwork. For all of these accomplishments, I am extremely grateful to Michael Gerber. Thanks to his teachings, Studio 904 has finally reached the point where it can now be called a turnkey business that can operate successfully without me.

CHAPTER 21:

IT'S MY WAY OR THE HIGHWAY

I hated placing want ads to recruit stylists in our local newspaper, *The Seattle Times*, because I rarely got the type of person I was looking to hire at my salon. Sure, I was picky, but not overly so. I just wanted someone who had the necessary skills, a professional appearance, and a pleasant personality. Was that too much to ask? Instead, the people who showed up for interviews usually wore open-toed sandals and had a disheveled look about them. Their hair resembled the radical styles featured in beauty magazines, with gaudy, colored streaks sweeping across their foreheads.

I typically began my interviews by asking "Can you tell me what your goals are for your career in the cosmetology industry?"

"I want to start making money right away so I can buy a new car," they often said. "I read somewhere that people in the industry can buy a Mercedes or a BMW after working for only a year."

"What do you think our work is all about?" I asked, in return.

"I want to do some trendy haircuts and colors like you see in *Modern Salon* magazine. I don't want to do the everyday, boring looks, but want to do... you know... stuff like red and blue streaks."

I would show them the *Book of Kaizen* and the details around my skill-certification training program, but very few seemed interested. Most of my would-be stylists kept their questions focused solely on money and tips. Rarely did any one mention the clients and making sure they were happy.

During one hiring cycle, the third stylist I interviewed appeared to be a step above almost everyone else I had previously interviewed. She was ten minutes early for her 11:00 a.m. appointment and looked very trendy, without being overly made up. Her make-up was polished and highlighted her porcelain skin and dark eyes. She smiled often, and when she did, her ruby-colored lips seemed to flicker.

The candidate's name was Melody. After I introduced myself, she said, "I've heard a lot about your salon's Kaizen philosophy of lifelong learning and I've always wanted to work for you. Your stylists think of themselves as a team, too, and I know that Studio 904 has awesome community service programs."

After I introduced myself, she said, "I've heard a lot about your salon and I've always wanted to work for you. I have heard a little bit about your salon's Kaizen philosophy of lifelong learning. You and your stylists think of yourselves as a team, too, and I've heard that Studio 904 has awesome community service programs."

It was so refreshing to hear these words spoken with such enthusiasm.

"I want to work here because I'm tired of working in a competitive environment where everyone works on commission and stabs each other in the back to protect their own client base. It's awful! I want to work in a stable salon where I can be part of a team with good pay and benefits," Melody finished.

"You came from a well-known salon in downtown Seattle," I said. What kind of wage were you making? I will try to match what you made last year if you can show me your W-2 form."

Melody hesitated a bit. "Sorry, I won't be able to do that," she said. "It was crazy! I made lots of money during the holiday season, but afterwards, I didn't even have enough to pay my rent. Besides, some of it was paid under the table."

"Really?" I remarked quizzically, before I could stop myself. In my mind, I knew that I would never consider the dishonest business practice of paying someone "under the table" and quickly changed the subject. "Melody, you mentioned that you had heard about the salon's Kaizen philosophy of lifelong learning, but have you heard about our *Book of Kaizen*?"

"I didn't know you had a book about it," Melody said.

"It explains everything from haircutting to coloring and styling, but more than that, it teaches how to live your life as a good community citizen."

"I'm all in for things like that!" she said quickly, "and I know that I can positively contribute to this salon."

"Yes, I think you can bring a lot to the salon with the skills you have. And if you are a fast learner, you should be able to quickly advance through our skill-certification system," I added.

"By the way," Melody said, "I was a color specialist and trainer at my previous salon. I hope you will consider me for work in your color department."

"You only want to do color services?" I inquired.

"Yes, that's my specialty. I've received tons of color education from national beauty leaders, and as the color lead at my old salon, I had two other stylists who worked under me," she replied.

"The salon you worked for was that specialized?" I asked.

"Yes. Is your salon departmentalized into haircutting and chemical services?" she asked.

"No, it isn't, I responded. I've asked every stylist to train in all the services that we offer our clients. In the end, they become top-notch, well-rounded stylists who can handle everything."

"If you give me a chance, I can show you how having a color specialist like me on your staff can give you more quality control," she said.

Melody seemed to know exactly what to say to keep my attention. I was thinking to myself that I would do anything to avoid getting phone calls from customers who were disappointed with the results of their hair color. Maybe Melody was onto something that just might work at the salon.

"What do you think about our *Book of Kaizen* and the training you would have to go through," I asked, returning the conversation to familiar ground.

Melody thought for a long minute. "I'm thinking that I would be happy to go through all the training your salon offers, with the exception of the color training. And, I'm confident I can spare you that cost and start on the floor right away. Let me show you what I can do."

I was a bit uncertain. A cautious voice in my head reminded me that I wanted to take every staff member through my own certification program – without *any* exceptions. But, having Melody earning income for the salon right away could be a huge boost. I was doing so much training and needed a break! On the other hand, my customers deserved well-trained staff members, I reminded myself. I was supposed to personally train every one of them to meet my high standards, but maybe this situation was different and deserved a trial. Excited at the possibilities, I took a gamble and called Melody back that same afternoon and offered her a job.

On her first day, Melody reported to work looking like a fashion model. I was proud to introduce her as our newest team member and gave a glowing review to our clients. The other team members heard my effusive comments throughout the morning and I am sure that they probably resented her immediately.

In the afternoon, I scheduled Melody for a foil weave with Mrs.

Diamond, a long-time client who was always asking us to do something new with her hair. Intrigued with the possibilities, I was sure that my newest stylist could give her an exciting new color. We put Melody's color tray together with precisely cut foil paper, glass color bowls, and a brand new application brush. I gushed to Mrs. Diamond about how much I was looking forward to seeing her new hair color.

I was in the back room training one of my other new stylists on the technique for doing airwave styling. "You can build fullness for a client with fine hair by pushing up the hair gently and blow drying the root area using your fingers," I told her. "See how softly I am blowing the hair?"

With a concerned look on her face, Jennie, one of the other stylists, abruptly interrupted us.

"Ummm... Kay, can you come out onto the floor and see what the new girl, Melody, is doing to Mrs. Diamond's hair?" she said.

I went quickly to that area of the salon and stopped dead in my tracks. Melody had Mrs. Diamond's hair sectioned off in big chunks and was applying a thick, bleach formula. The foil weave was exactly the opposite of the salon's color philosophy of using natural and healthy hair coloring. The color was absolutely too dramatic and too bold. I wanted to immediately stop the service but I couldn't approach both of them without alarming the client. Feeling helpless, I convinced myself that Melody knew what she was doing. I tried to assure myself that it was a new technique that I wasn't aware of and that everything was going to be fine.

A short while later, I heard the water being turned on at the shampoo bowl as Melody took out Mrs. Diamond's foils. There was the sound of swishing water, followed by the blow dryer as Melody started drying and styling her client's hair.

There were a few minutes of silence.

Then, I heard Mrs. Diamond gasp and yell, "What did you do to my hair? I look like a striped tiger!"

I ran out onto the floor to find two of my stylists huddled in the corner, looking horrified. All the clients in the salon were staring at Melody, but particularly at Mrs. Diamond. Her hair was vibrantly striped and almost orange. I was mortified.

Mrs. Diamond jumped up from the salon chair and ripped off her cape, completely enraged. I heard her sobbing and screaming "What have you done to my hair?" as she started running out of the salon.

I was close behind, offering countless apologies along the way. All afternoon, I tried to reach her on the phone. She refused to answer my calls and I never saw her again. I couldn't blame her because I had vastly over-promised and terribly under-delivered with my new stylist. Thinking back, I still feel guilty about that situation and wish that I had been given the chance to fix her hair myself.

Following the day's disaster, I immediately called Melody into my office for a serious talk. After her first dreadful attempt at color, I recommended that she go through Studio 904's color and foil training. She steadfastly refused and subsequently gave her notice to quit. We said our goodbyes at the front door and I watched as she walked away into the rainy streets of downtown Seattle. Even with what had happened, I was definitely torn because there was something in me that didn't want to let her go. With the proper training and a little more openness to learning new techniques, I thought that she had the skills to become one of the better stylists in the industry. It was a shame that her ego got in the way of learning and growing; it definitely kept her from reaching her full potential.

I learned a valuable lesson that day. Going forward, I would not give into the temptation to get faster results by eliminating any phase of the training for my stylists. Melody's experience was often brought up as an example of what could happen if the training wasn't done completely and consistently. Like Melody, many of the stylists I hired, brought their own personal idiosyncrasies that they had picked up from other salons or their school training. In order to ensure their success, it was often necessary for me to exercise a certain measure of "tough love" to drive home important points. I continually reinforced that our clients deserved skill-certified stylists when they came into our salon and that the bottom line had to be "my way or the highway" if we were all going to succeed.

CHAPTER 22:

YOU'RE LOOKING GOOD!

Shortly after I started my business, I created a community service program called "You're Looking Good!" The goal of the program was to give haircuts and styles to students attending elementary schools in the Rainier Valley area of Seattle who couldn't afford to get their hair done professionally. Basically, anyone on a subsidized meal program was eligible to participate.

Every time we went to a school, I closed the salon for at least three hours. All of the stylists participated and were paid their regular salaries. The combination of reduced business hours at the salon plus supporting a full payroll was financially difficult, but I was committed to giving back to the community.

While contemplating the program, I asked myself a hundred questions: "Who do you think you are?" "What makes your small business so special you can do something like this?" "How will you ever be able to afford such a program?"

Determined to make this work, I stuck to my convictions and told myself "I'm only a small business and I won't be able to make a huge difference in a person's life, but it's important for me to touch those who need a helping hand - even if it is only in a small way."

But why low-income children? They or their parents would probably never become clients at Studio 904. As I developed the program, I often asked myself, "Why can't you be more strategic? You should be picking your community-service projects in ways that will help your salon be more profitable, not cost you more money."

My eventual answer was, "I want myself and my stylists to become better human beings. My business should encompass humility, humbleness, and empathy. I want to associate with others who want to accomplish small, but meaningful changes in our community."

Luckily, I met a like-minded person in Susan McCormick, the principal of Whitworth Elementary School. I had never met an educator so dedicated to her students. Susan stood outside on the sidewalk every morning and welcomed each student to school with a smile. She knew each one by name and was the resident cheerleader for all of her students. For instance, when Jim came to school looking grumpy or sad, she would put her hand his shoulder and say "Jim, we're going to have a good day today, aren't we?" She would look at him until he responded with a smile. "That's a good; now go get 'em!" she would say, as he hurried off to class. Everyone always left her presence in a good mood.

"I cheer them on because some of them have little reason to be happy in their lives," Susan explained to me. "They tolerate abusive home situations, live with unemployed parents, and often come to school hungry. I need to make sure that their stomachs are full and that they are happy and ready to learn. We can try to teach them all we want, but it's futile unless their basic needs are taken care of first. The challenging environment that most of these kids live in is the reason why I really appreciate your monthly visit to our school to cut and style their hair," she continued. "It helps them feel good about themselves to be well-groomed. You are a real hero, which is an unusual title for most business owners."

For my part, I thought the real heroes were the kids who were in our "You're Looking Good" haircutting program – scores of kids who were often struggling in school, facing poverty and neglect, or in dire need of attention, yet somehow managing to survive.

Here's how one of our school visits typically went: After the school bell rang to signal the end of breakfast, my stylists and I headed to the lunchroom. The air smelled like sausages, pancakes, and syrup when we entered. Eager to help, my three stylists organized the students into separate rows on the floor. They were excited and noisy, but their enthusiastic shout of "Good morning!" gave me confidence that we were going to have a great day.

"We are glad to be here again," I told them from the front of the room. "My stylists and I do this because we want you to have a good hair day. You never feel very good about yourself when you're having a bad hair day, do you? We want you to have a good hair day *every* day."

One of the boys suddenly stood up and pointed to an African-American girl named Darlene, who had unusually kinky hair. "Yeah, we don't want to look like her!" he shouted. "She has a bad hair day every day!"

Susan was furious, but in control. "Stop that Mark! That was a very rude thing to say to Darlene!" she said, in a raised voice. "Please go over and apologize to her *right now*!"

I was horrified to see Darlene sitting there with tears rolling down her face. After I moved to the United States from Japan, I distinctly remember getting similarly teased in my class – all because I didn't speak a word of English. I was singled out because I was different and now that painful moment was unfolding with someone else right before my eyes.

Quickly walking over to the shy, little girl, I gave her a big hug. "Don't worry," I said. "We will have you looking so good that no one will ever say that to you again. I promise."

We shampooed, cut, and styled Darlene's hair and left her with a beauty kit that contained a brush, comb, flowered barrettes, and a good hair cream. We taught her what to do at home to keep her hair healthy and looking good. She gave us a big grin at the end and a gorgeous face emerged, showing off her big, sparkly eyes and shiny skin. I carefully pinned a black "You're Looking Good!" button to her blouse and she joyfully skipped out of the lunchroom to her class.

Susan called me that afternoon. "Kay, I just had to call and tell you that Darlene was so happy after your visit!" she exclaimed. "I don't know if she has ever received that kind of attention before, but her joy was so infectious that she made everyone around her happy, too!"

Soon, there were more kids who wanted their hair cut. When my staff and I couldn't attend to all of the students, Susan would drive her students to our Pioneer Square salon in the school van. It created quite a commotion when they came barreling through our front door and into our design area during normal business hours. I am sure that some of the clients were amused and others were probably wondering why I was cutting these school children's hair. After the experiences I had with kids like Darlene, however, I knew in my heart that it was the right thing to do.

A few weeks later, I was invited to attend a function at Beacon Hill Elementary School, another school in a lower-income part of Seattle where my team and I often visited to give haircuts to the students.

"I don't know if you know this," a teacher said breathlessly on the phone, "but Governor Gary Locke attended our school as a child and has decided to come back and pay us a visit." Almost unable to contain herself, I could imagine her jumping up and down at the end of the line as we were talking.

But I'm not a student or a teacher. "Why me?" I asked.

"Why not you? With all that you've done to help our school, it wouldn't be right if you weren't here to celebrate the Governor's visit with us," she replied.

The school was buzzing with anticipation when I entered. The hallways were decorated with red, white, and blue crepe paper streamers and a large "Welcome, Governor Gary Locke" banner hung at the entrance. First-through-sixth grade students were lined up outside the assembly room.

One of the teachers led me to the front of the line of students and all of a sudden, loud cheering broke out. I turned around, looking for the Governor, only to discover that the students were cheering for *me*!

"Thank you Studio 904! I like my haircut!" they yelled. "Please come again!" Some of them reached out to grab my hand.

The school's principal walked up to me and said, "I should have known! You are more popular than the Governor!"

I couldn't imagine feeling any happier or prouder than I was during that moment.

As word about my community service program in the schools spread, John Franco, a steadfast client of my salon over the years, eagerly stepped forward. John was the president of the local Rainier Valley Rotary Club. With his encouragement, his members presented a generous check for $1,000 to help fund my program. I gratefully accepted it and combined it with some additional monies that had been donated by our product manufacturers. With the donated funds, we were able to put together five-hundred hygiene and personal care kits. The kits included items such as hair brushes, shampoo, and lotion. With everyone's help, "You're Looking Good!" continued for six years, touching hundreds of students attending schools in the Seattle area. Reflecting on the excitement and joy in the students' faces over all those years reinforced in me that I had made the right decision to find a way to give back.

In addition to the warm feeling that my stylists and I had after every visit, we made new and special friends, built a solid reputation for being a good neighbor, and contributed to improving the welfare of people in the surrounding communities.

I never intended for our efforts to translate directly into tangible dollars, but I believe that the overwhelming support and appreciation we received in return is one of the reasons that Studio 904 has sustained itself over the last forty years.

And that in itself is reward enough.

CHAPTER 23:

STUDENTS AS MY TEACHERS

On every page of the local Sunday newspaper, there are always large, blaring ads selling items from supermarkets and department stores to lawyer's services and enrollment in specialized pre-schools. Everyone who still reads a newspaper knows what I am talking about. I hated seeing all of those ads and never wanted to be a part of that kind of mainstream advertising.

What I wanted was something unique and worthwhile - advertising that contained a special message to attract the kinds of clients who were right for us, namely customers who were socially conscious and interested in positive change. It may have been somewhat idealistic, but I wanted to talk to them about things that mattered in the world instead of engaging in endless, mindless chatter all of the time. Any business, even a small one like mine, can reach hundreds of people in a month. Through this extensive reach, I believe that a business has the potential to change attitudes and behaviors by taking advantage of opportunities to educate its customers and raise their awareness of important social issues.

Even though I was certain about what I believed in, I couldn't find any other business owner who felt the same way. A number of people called me a "Pollyanna." "You can't operate a successful business thinking the world is some idyllic place," people would tell me. "It's a dog-eat-dog world and if you don't wake up to that fact, you'll be eaten alive." After receiving a steady dose of these types of sentiments, I didn't know who to turn to. I also questioned whether I should be operating a salon or any other kind of business if this was the prevailing attitude of business owners.

Fortunately, one day I read a small notice in the local paper from Dr. Harriet Stephenson of Seattle University's Business Program. The announcement read: "Students from Seattle University are interested in connecting with small business owners who operate socially-responsible businesses. In this three-month program, the student teams will meet with the business owners on a weekly basis. Their goal is to create a sustainable plan for the business. At the end of the program, each team will present their findings to the class. Dr. Stephenson will grade each project." At first, I was a bit skeptical. Then, I thought, "I have nothing to lose, so why not send in an application?"

A few months went by and I had forgotten all about my application. Then, one day, I reached into my mailbox and noticed a large, manila envelope with a return address of Seattle University. Inside, the cover letter stated that my business had been chosen by one of the student teams! I was excited and quickly read the details. The letter stated that an individual team would consist of five students, who would each focus on a specific subject area, i.e., human resources, marketing, finance, operations and strategic planning, and leadership. I needed help in all of those areas, so it looked really promising.

Within a week, the team and I made arrangements to meet for the first time. Our meeting was very stimulating, with lots of interaction between myself and the students. After our session concluded, I was overwhelmed with the number of questions they had. Many of the questions I had asked myself over the years, but had never verbalized the answers out loud to anyone. One of the first questions they asked was, "Why did you decide to open a business?" Followed by, "What is your vision? Are you happy with how your business is doing? What are some of your challenges? How are you doing financially? Do you have enough customers? Who are your clients and what is your retention rate?" And on and on they went. Someone requested my profit and loss statement, balance sheet, and cash-flow reports. Another student wanted all of my policies, job descriptions, marketing history, and customer service procedures. Although they were all excellent questions, I couldn't help but be protective. After all, at the time, I hardly knew any of these kids.

A week later, any low expectations that I had were quickly eliminated when they presented me with a professionally-written report; it included a summarized analysis that was based on my responses to their questions, as well as the papers and reports I had given them. As they summarized each section for me, I couldn't help but be impressed with how they had managed to articulate all of the challenges that I faced.

Thrilled with the quality of their input, I found myself looking forward to their visits. Most times, we would sit in my back office for hours, drinking tea and coffee while talking about what a socially-responsible and sustainable business would look like and how to build a foundation that would help me get there. The students even put together a survey and called all of my Studio 904 customers to get their feedback.

After all of the basic operational issues were addressed, it was finally time to discuss my marketing program.

"We know that you have a personal preference as to how you'd like to market your salon. Can you tell us why and what you have in mind?" one of the students asked.

"Well, I've never felt good about taking money from our clients and not giving any of it back to the community to help people who are in need."

"But, what if you needed the money to keep your business going and didn't have any excess funds to contribute?" someone inquired.

"Yes," I said, feeling rather unrealistic. "I know it sounds kind of reckless, but a while back I heard Mother Teresa say something that resonated all the way to my inner core. She said, "most people give from the point of surplus, but the true meaning of giving is to give from the point of wanting."

The room fell silent.

"When I ask people to donate to a cause," I continued, "they say that they would like to, but they can't afford it. I often find that hard to believe when I see these same people spending money on frivolous things like expensive coffee drinks, brand name purses, and all the rest. I always want to say to them, "If you can spend $20 on yourself, surely you can give a dollar or two toward helping others."

Looking into their eyes and noticing their body language, I could see that I was connecting with the students on an emotional level; they were seriously listening to what I had to say. For the first time, I finally felt like someone was actually *hearing* my message.

I continued on. "I believe that a business is a powerful tool for education and empathy. We hear all about the desperation in the world through reading newspapers and watching TV, but it doesn't force us to take action. A business is a powerful vehicle where we can communicate with our clients in a way that tugs directly at their heartstrings and makes it easy for them to donate to a cause. I don't want them to feel like they have to donate large amounts of money. For example, a small business like mine could easily attract 800 clients through our door in a given month. If each one buys a $5 raffle ticket to enter a drawing, small prizes could be donated and awarded to a few winners, while thousands of dollars would be raised to support a specific cause."

"That would be $4,000!" exclaimed Susan, one of the students, who jumped out of her chair with eyes wide open.

"Exactly. And doing this small act of kindness makes our clients feel good about themselves too. I can see it in their eyes when they realize that their contribution is going toward a good cause that helps people or animals that need help," I said, with my face breaking out in a big smile.

Everyone else in the room quickly rose to their feet and there was suddenly an electric air of excitement in the room.

"Wow!" said Alex, another student. "This is really enlightening. In school, we learn that businesses must make money in order to survive, but they don't put nearly as much emphasis on the opportunities that businesses have to create a better world. To see first-hand how this could work in the real world is so important and pretty impressive."

"I got it! We will call Studio 904's new promotion "Gratitude Marketing!" shouted Mary, one of the marketing students. "Let's go out onto the design floor and remove all of the beauty product signs. We can replace them with fundraising notices!" As clients and employees looked on, we quickly marched out to the front of the salon and celebrated our new campaign by removing all of the product advertisements from the mirrors and walls.

Two months later, the student team presented their Studio 904 Business Plan to their fellow classmates and Dr. Stephenson. I was not only incredibly proud of them, but also grateful for their recommendations and what they had done to improve my business. As I was leaving the campus after the presentation, Dr. Stephenson rushed after me to say, "Kay, I want to thank you very much for working with my students. You lit a fire under them. They were energized and engaged during the three months they spent with you and they did a fine job on their project. "Dr. Stephenson," I replied, "I don't think you realize how much I learned from them! They gave me the confidence to move forward with a unique business model that I can hardly wait to implement."

Upon returning to my salon, it suddenly felt very empty without all of the students around. Over the course of the next few weeks, I worked hard to carry out their recommendations, but I missed interacting directly with them on a regular basis. It was like losing several valuable members of my team.

It didn't last long, however, as I soon received a phone call from Alex, a member of the student team. He asked me if there was a possible opening for a general manager position at Studio 904. Of course, I hired him. For two years, his contributions and optimistic energy were invaluable to the success of the salon.

Over the years, I wrote recommendation letters for several of the students in the class. As I wrote each letter, I distinctly remembered how they had helped me to create the idea behind "Gratitude Marketing" and how the idea had now become a high priority in not only my business, but other businesses, big and small. To create that kind of impact with a simple idea and a lot of passion was life changing for me; I am indeed indebted to the inspiration the students provided when I needed it the most.

A few years later, I received an invitation from the students at Seattle University to be a speaker for a Tedx talk event.

WATCH MY VIDEO:

Chapter 23: Students As My Teachers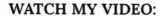

http://keikokayhirai.com/chapter-23-students-as-my-teachers/

CHAPTER 24:

LEADERS WHO INSPIRED ME

As I built my business, daily inspirations came from many people I admired along the way. Some are household names, while others are unfamiliar to most. All, however, were equally important in the positive impact they had on my life. Some were business leaders who just happened to be clients of Studio 904. Others were people who I had the privilege to work with in numerous volunteer organizations. I have always been intrigued with watching trailblazers and wanted to learn more about what made them successful. Studying how they made their decisions, how they interacted with other individuals, and the manner in which they moved and inspired people around them was a fascination of mine. Let me share with you what I learned from three of those people I had the good fortune to meet:

Howard Schultz, the Chairman and CEO of Starbucks, is a person with a definite long-term vision. When I first met Howard, his dream was to show the world that coffee could be enjoyed by the cup. He believed that enjoying a cup of coffee could be the impetus for meeting with friends or colleagues in an intimate and pleasing environment. At the time, his epiphany was way ahead of its time. When Howard came to the salon for his monthly haircut, I always made a point of asking him how his efforts were coming along to raise the capital he needed to develop a chain of coffee shops. As he sat down one late afternoon, ready to get his hair cut, he appeared weary from his day's activities.

"Howard, how is your fundraising going?" I asked.

"I played basketball with potential funders today and I talked to them about my idea of selling coffee by the cup. I'm not sure how seriously they took it, though," he replied.

"Do you sometimes feel like just giving up?" I asked, feeling badly for him.

"No Kay, I don't. I have to keep on going."

"How do you go about doing that day after day, Howard? It must get so discouraging for you," I replied.

"Well, you just have to keep forging ahead, regardless," he responded, while gently nodding his head.

I decided that it was better not to prolong this particular discussion and finished cutting his hair.

The next time he came into the salon, Howard had a little paperback book in his hand. "Remember you asked me how I keep going? Well, I have a gift for you," he said, as he handed me the book. The book's title was: *"Jacob's Journey, Wisdom to Find the Way, Strength to Carry On."* The author's name was Noah benShea. As I am writing this chapter of my book, Howard's gift sits next to my computer. The edges of the book's pages have turned yellow with age, but the teachings inside continue to be an inspiration to me every day. I am so pleased that Howard Schultz eventually realized his initial vision and subsequently built a worldwide coffee empire - an accomplishment that went far beyond his wildest dreams when he first set out. Aside from his financial success, however, I believe that the best thing he has done is to bring about an awareness of social causes in his business model. In my opinion, it is what makes Starbucks not only a good company, but a great one.

When I first met **Mary Gates**, she was a successful community leader and philanthropist, but was probably better-known for being the wife of Bill Gates, Senior, a prominent local attorney, and the mother of a remarkable son named Bill Gates, Junior, the founder of Microsoft. Aside from her numerous activities, she was also heavily involved with many community programs that served underprivileged groups in Seattle. Over the years, Mary and I had many wonderful conversations when she came to visit my salon.

One day, as she sat in my chair to have her hair styled, she said to me, "Is it okay if I vent a little to you? After I say what I'm going to say, can we call it "done," so that we can go on to talk about other things?"

"Sure, Mary," I replied.

"I'm really bothered about this, but I don't know how to handle it," she said, looking at me in the mirror.

"Okay, go ahead," I said.

"It's my son Bill's birthday this weekend and I planned a party for him at my home. I invited thirty people and they all accepted my invitation to attend," she said.

"Wow! That sounds like it is going to be a wonderful event. Bill is lucky to have a mother like you," I responded.

"Well, you won't believe this. He had the gall to call me up today to say that he won't be attending. What will I tell the guests? How can I have a party without the guest of honor?" she asked.

"Why did he say that he won't he be coming, Mary?" I inquired.

"He said he had an important management team meeting on

Monday morning and he had to stay at home to prepare the agenda. He said that devoting the time and energy to constructing the agenda is a key to having a successful meeting. Can you believe that?" she said, in disbelief.

Mary was so diplomatic, though. I could tell that she just wanted to air this minor annoyance to someone who would listen. "Thanks for hearing me out," she said, ready to move on. "Now let's talk about something else. No use wasting time on things that I don't have any control over." As she held up her hands and responded with resignation, she concluded, "I guess Bill is just who he is and I can't change that."

I responded with a big smile on my face, "Mary, *you* are the reason why Bill Gates and Microsoft are so great! I know that deep down you are so proud of him and his accomplishments! And you should be!"

Looking back, I learned something very important from my conversation with Mary that day. From her son's comments, I realized the importance of preparing detailed agendas for my meetings that included the topics to be discussed as well as the potential outcomes that I wanted to see at its conclusion. I also realized that entrepreneurs, like Bill Gates, sometimes have to make important, personal sacrifices in order to reach their ultimate goal.

Being a chairperson for the governor's Small Business Improvement Council was not an easy task. I traveled to Olympia once a month and conducted meetings with small business owners from all corners of the state of Washington. In addition, representatives from government agencies attended our meetings, so there was always a captive audience. Small business members eagerly participated to share their ideas on how government could improve their economic vitality.

One day, I was conducting a meeting in one of the large board rooms in the Capitol building. With everyone seated and Governor Mike Lowry at the head of the table, a door suddenly flung open. As we all looked, state representative **Dawn Mason**, an imposing, African-American woman, entered the room and quickly sat down at the table. She was given a proper introduction and the meeting resumed.

A few minutes later, Dawn raised her hand and made an observation to Governor Lowry, "Governor, if this group is representative of small business owners throughout our state, then something is wrong."

"What's wrong, Representative Mason?" asked Governor Lowry.

"How come there are no minorities in this room except for Kay and me?"

The room fell eerily silent and all eyes were fixated on Representative Mason and me.

"To answer your question, I want to tell you that we have tried to find minority-owned businesses, but have been unsuccessful in spite of our efforts," replied Governor Lowry.

Dawn Mason looked him squarely in the eyes and said, "How hard did you try?"

As the chair of the board, I knew I had to do something to ease the tension, so I said, "Representative Mason, I'd be happy to get together with you after the meeting so we can discuss how we might recruit more minority-owned businesses to this board."

I will never forget Representative Dawn Mason. Something about her standing up to voice her beliefs and having the fortitude to bring them to the forefront really appealed to me. Truth be known, I admired her because she possessed the guts that I wished I had.

As time went on, I got to know Dawn Mason better when I had the opportunity to drive with her to Eastern Washington to attend other meetings for the Council. While there, we learned so much about the challenges that faced small rural businesses - challenges that are very different from their large, urban counterparts. It was a daily struggle for them to keep their agricultural and retail economy healthy and to provide a living wage for their employees. On one of the last trips we took together, Dawn and I became involved in a serious discussion about lifelong learning.

I asked her, "Who influenced your commitment to lifelong learning?"

"My Mother, who was so wise, she replied. "Let me share with you what my dear Mother told me. She told me that you can learn something from anything you come in contact with. If you sit alone on a river bank and stare at a rock long enough, you will learn something from it." I was deeply touched by this sentiment and often referred to it when I taught my students and employees about the power of continuous learning throughout one's life.

These are the stories of just three people who have positively impacted my life. There are many more. As I reflect back on my life's journey, I am grateful that these and others, through one set of circumstances or another, somehow crossed my path while on their own personal journeys. I am sure that all of you have a similar group of influencers that have made a significant contribution to how you view the world and live your life. My daily goal is to find ways that I can make someone's life better. It is my way of giving back and expressing my gratitude for those who have shared their wisdom with me and helped me along the way; it's the least I can do.

CHAPTER 25:

DO YOU HAVE A MENTOR?

If you don't have a mentor right now, you might think about starting a search for one. Why? Because chances are, if you find someone who is a good fit for your personality and lifestyle, you will be able to live your life with more confidence and the reassurance that you are headed in the right direction toward fulfilling your life goals. What is my definition of a suitable mentor? A mentor is generally someone who:

- Has a higher understanding or knowledge than you do either in life experiences, in a certain area of expertise, or both

- Shares your values and expectations

- You admire

- You feel comfortable with to share your inner-most feelings

If you find someone who fits this description and is willing to spend the time with you, either as a friend or as an advisor, consider yourself very lucky.

I feel very fortunate because I have a wonderful mentor named Joe Greengard. Joe is someone whom I admire and respect. I first became friends with Joe's wife, Lila. She was an early client of Studio 904 and we have been good friends since our initial meeting. When I  subsequently met Joe, he was busy running a clothing manufacturing business in Seattle and had little time for anything else. If I had asked him to be my mentor then, it probably would not have worked out. When he sold his business and had more time, I started thinking about approaching him to see if he would be available to give me advice on future planning, not only for my business, but also for my personal life.

Joe had owned a company named "Collectibles," so I was confident that I would be getting advice from a hard-working, successful small business owner. He had been in the trenches, learned the "ins and outs" of running a business, and provided realistic and pragmatic recommendations. His approach was in direct contrast to typical consultants who got many of their ideas and recommendations from reading business books and charged large sums of money for their services.

I considered calling Joe after a particularly frustrating evening of reviewing the financial statements for my business. Unfortunately, the sudden economic downturn and recent staffing problems had left my business in a pretty dismal state. I had cut out every business and personal expense I could think of, including my own paycheck. How much longer could I go on eating tuna fish sandwiches for dinner? The thought of eating another one of those cold sandwiches made my stomach turn.

Everyone has been through tough times in their life when they have had to reduce expenses, but I was having a hard time coming up with a viable way to balance not just *some* of my expenses, but *all* of my expenses to save my business. In a fit of desperation, I finally picked up the phone and dialed Joe's number. When he answered, I pleaded, "Joe, can you *please* help me? I *really* need your help."

After explaining my problem, Joe responded in his always cheerful voice, "Not to worry, Kay. Just send me your profit and loss statement and your balance sheet as soon as you can. After I look them over, we can meet and talk, okay?"

I thought to myself, Joe is so smart. More than that, he is calm, nice, and unassuming. He has a way of making people feel comfortable around him and I admired that. This personal characteristic was helpful because discussing my personal and business cash-flow problems with a stranger was intimidating and somewhat embarrassing. It didn't help, either, that I was a right-brained individual. Managing cash flow was something that didn't come naturally for me.

A few weeks after I called Joe and forwarded my financials to him, Joe came to the salon to discuss how to get my finances back in line.

"Joe, with my cash flow at an all-time low, I just don't know what else I can do," I said. As I sat complaining to him, I realized that I wasn't looking directly at Joe. Instead, my eyes were glancing down at the table because of the shame I felt for being in this difficult position.

Instead of giving in to my gloom and doom, Joe's eyes instantly lit up. He looked at me and said, "Kay, don't worry. I enjoy looking at numbers and solving problems and I already know that I can help you out of your deficit situation. Having looked over your financial statements, I can think of several things you can easily do in order to cut back on some of your expenses."

"What? Are you sure? I have spent a lot of hours looking at different things that I could cut back and I couldn't come up with anything else. I would really be surprised if you found something that I missed. By the way, one thing you should know is that I *refuse* to cut my employees' wages, so don't recommend anything along those lines," I said defiantly.

"It's okay and I understand where you are coming from. My wife, Lila, has been a long-time customer of your salon and she's told me how much each employee's well-being means to you," he said, using a soothing voice to calm me down.

"If you can find any other places where I can cut expenses, it would be a miracle," I replied.

"Kay, I'm looking at this line item "Facility Maintenance" at $500 per month. Can you tell me what that is for?"

"That's the fee I pay the cleaning crew to come in and clean the floors and other areas of the salon when they need a little sprucing up," I informed him.

Joe didn't say a word. He just stared at me to the point that I began to feel somewhat uncomfortable.

"Why are you looking at me like that Joe? I need to have the salon clean. Our customers don't want to come into a dirty, poorly maintained facility," I explained.

"Kay, we have to do what we have to do at times like this, don't we?" Joe responded.

"What do you mean? Are you saying that *I* should be the cleaning person?" I said.

"Yes, I bet you will do a wonderful job. You can ask your husband to help out, too," Joe suggested.

"Oh, my gosh! It's come down to this?" I asked, in disbelief.

"And don't forget to turn off all of your lights every evening. That will help your electrical bill, too," he said, with an impish smile.

His laser eyes spotted another line item under "Employee Meetings."

"I don't think it's necessary to feed your employees at every meeting," he suggested.

"I can't cut that out, Joe. They expect it," I replied.

"Kay, I'm sure they will understand when you explain to them that you need to find ways to tighten things up during this difficult time," he said.

Surprisingly, we ended the evening on a happy note. I actually got excited at the thought of being the cleaning lady until things improved with my business.

Using Joe's suggestions and cutting back on a variety of expenses did not bring my business back to a solid financial position right away. But, it certainly helped. What was more important in the long run was the advice that he gave me about understanding the basic elements of human nature. He taught me that, after a while, everyone gets stuck handling things in a specific way; people honestly believe that they can't change their normal way of thinking and working. Circumstances, however, sometimes force a person to see that there are different, more effective approaches to thinking and getting things accomplished.

Joe's sage advice at the time helped to create a new mindset in how I view and think about finances related to both my personal and business life. His continued guidance has convinced me that making small changes on a daily basis will eventually lead to bigger transformations down the road. In time, all of these roads will lead toward a better, more positive destination in one's life.

Even with all of the business connections that I had nurtured over the years of being in business, it was still difficult to find people who I trusted and had the necessary expertise to help guide me. That's why finding Joe has made such a difference in my life, both on a professional and a personal level. Early on, Joe helped me improve my day-to-day business operations. Later, he helped with strategic and long-term planning. I always loved getting Joe's phone calls suggesting, "Kay, lets meet for lunch soon and talk about how you are doing these days." After hearing my concerns and possible solutions, he never fails to say, "Now wait a minute, Kay! Before you give up on that, let's explore some other options!" He always finds the proverbial "little crack in the door opening where the light shines through," which I really appreciate about him.

Joe is physically fit, leads a disciplined life, and treats his family and everyone around him with the utmost kindness and respect. His mind is extremely sharp and he is always ready to help others solve problems. I hope you can find a "Joe" in your life. I so respect and value Joe. I hope you can find a "Joe" in your life.

CHAPTER 26:

MY IDEAS ARE CATCHING ON!

After a lot of hard work and effort, my Kaizen philosophy of "lifelong learning in small incremental steps," my unique approach to a team-based pay system, and my formal employee training programs were finally taking hold and showing some success. As my business was starting to turn the corner, I enjoyed my daily life of working at the salon and spending time in the community. I spent a lot of time helping the Pioneer Square Community Association cope with the many challenges that came its way. Numerous hours were spent every week to help the homeless who frequented this historic district on Seattle's waterfront. Time was also spent working with the mayor's office, thinking of ways to improve the Pioneer Square district and attract new businesses. We worked diligently to create a business district that would thrive alongside a new baseball stadium that was being built. After reviewing the stadium plans, we knew that it was going to have a major impact on our district, and we wanted to make sure that we could attract businesses that would cohesively blend in without changing our unique character.

Meanwhile, my business methods and community outreach programs were slowly starting to catch the eye of business leaders. I received many personal awards associated with Studio 904, including the Better Business Bureau International Award for Marketplace Ethics; the Minority Entrepreneur Business of the Year, which was sponsored by the Washington State Department of Labor and Industries; and the Small Business Association's Hero Award. Extremely proud and humbled by the honors, I traveled all over the United States to attend the various award ceremonies.

As a small business owner, however, I was not always comfortable getting all of this attention and often wondered, "Why me?" I got especially nervous when news reporters came to interview me and take my picture. And then to see the articles and stories come out in the various news media the following day was almost surreal. I had never experienced anything like that before. This kind of immediate visibility, however, had a positive snowball effect on every aspect of my business. People from throughout the community came to get their hair done and potential employees sought us out to work at the salon. It gave me hope that I was finally doing the right things.

As I walked through the styling area of the salon, I was often approached by customers who rushed up to me and asked, "Are you Kay?"

"Yes, I am. What can I do for you?"

"I heard you have a unique philosophy for running your salon," they said. "Can you tell me about it?"

Often, I had to ask myself if I was hearing their requests correctly. All of these people wanted to hear about my innermost passions and about my philosophy for running the salon? Of course, I was flattered to answer their questions. I was amazed that telling my story over and over again to people actually validated what I had always believed in, deep down in my soul.

Getting so much recognition in the community, however, also created extra pressure on me. I sometimes felt that everyone who came to our salon expected something more than what I thought we could deliver and I began to feel like an imposter who didn't deserve all of the accolades and awards. To counter those thoughts, I decided to augment our existing training program. All of the stylists got skill-certified in giving haircuts and foil weaves and working together as a team. In addition, everyone was taught enhanced customer service skills that included in-depth skills for effectively consulting with clients.

It paid off. Looking out on the salon floor one afternoon, I was happy to see a customer sitting in one of our chairs, relaxed and snoozing as Renee meticulously wrapped her hair in foil pieces. Then, I saw Renee step away to tend to another client. With perfect timing, Steve stepped in and took over the foil service. When he finished wrapping the last piece of foil, he said softly to the client, "Mary, I'm finished wrapping your last foil weave. I'll check back with you in ten minutes." The client looked up with a surprised expression on her face as she said, "Oh, when did you step in Steve? I didn't even know that a switch had been made," she said.

I immediately pulled Renee and Steve to the dispensary room and exclaimed, "Congratulations to both of you for making such a flawless transition with Mary! She was not even aware that you, Renee, had left and that you, Steve, had stepped in. Your procedures and touch were so smooth and similar that the customer had no idea that the two of you had just performed the perfect waltz!"

Witnessing such efficiency by my team members made me feel good. Not only did we become more productive in delivering services, but our customers loved leaving the salon in a timely manner. I knew that this approach was exactly what Dr. Deming, the main catalyst behind the incredible industry success in Japan, meant when he said, "When you improve quality, you automatically improve productivity."

I was surprised and flattered when I got a call from the director of the Washington Medical Association one day. He wanted me to lead a workshop on my Kaizen-inspired business management system at their annual meeting of hospital leaders. After receiving a standing ovation following my presentation, I realized that my business philosophy and its quality assurance procedures not only worked for hair salons, but were applicable to all businesses, including the medical profession.

Even with all of the exposure that we received in the television and print media, I was disappointed that none of the big name salons in the city had ever approached me to ask what I was doing. The only explanation that I could come up with was that the cosmetology industry was standing firm behind their long-held policy of commissioned hair stylists and chair rentals and were reluctant to adopt anything new.

My spirits were lifted one afternoon, however, when I received a phone call from a salon owner in Vancouver, Washington.

"Hi, Kay. My name is Noreen, she said. I heard about your salon and am intrigued with your system of employee training and teamwork. If you are amenable to a meeting, two other salon owners and myself would like to make an appointment to learn about how you are running your salon," she said.

"Yes, I'd love to talk to you and your friends," I replied.

Two days later, Noreen, Claudia, and Beth made the four-hour drive to Seattle and spent the afternoon in my salon.

After I gave them a tour of the salon and introduced them to my stylists, they were excited to sit down in my office and start interviewing me. But first, I asked, "Besides seeing my salon, what is the main purpose of your visit today?"

Noreen, who was the spokesperson for the group, got the conversation rolling. "Kay, we're here because we are frustrated with how our salons are doing. One of our main problems is that there is a constant turnover of staff. With most of the staff doing their own thing, it is difficult to keep a regular group of customers coming to our salons. We seem to be constantly spinning our wheels and can't seem to get ahead."

As soon as Noreen finished, Claudia piped in, "I'm in a worse situation than Noreen. I had to close the door to my salon and spa last week. I'm now out of business."

"What happened?" I asked.

"I had my entire staff walk out of the salon. They got upset with how things were being run, created a big drama within the salon, and then, poof, they all left. I walked into an empty salon the next morning with my customers standing outside the door," she said, with tears streaming down her face.

The third woman, Jane, echoed what Noreen had said. "I feel like I don't even own my business," she explained. The salon is driven by what the stylists want to do. They dictate the kind of music they want to hear and the products they want to use. They have no clue what the customers want."

Each of the women complained about the same things that I used to complain about when I opened my first salon. Listening to what they were saying made me realize how good I had it and how much I loved coming to work. It was something I was excited about and sincerely looked forward to each day as I stepped through the door.

The meeting turned out to be very productive and beneficial for everyone, so I met Noreen and a group of salon owners on a pretty regular basis to share our thoughts on business practices like salary pay, team training, and financial management systems. As word got out, this small number of salon owners expanded quickly. Before I knew it, I was talking with salon owners in many small, outlying areas of Washington State.

Over the course of these meetings, Noreen and I became good friends and traveled to many workshops and trade shows together. Her gutsy style and adventurous personality increased the joy in running my business and living my life.

Although my business was doing well and I enjoyed my association with other like-minded salon owners, the same could not be said about my daughter, Sheri. Dr. Reeves, a well-known pediatrician, had been overseeing her rehabilitation after she sustained a traumatic head injury while walking home from school. About a year after Sheri's accident, we had a routine office visit with the doctor. Usually a friendly encounter, our discussion soon turned tense and emotional.

"Well, Tommy and Kay, how are things going for Sheri at school?" he asked.

I twisted my hands nervously and said, "Dr. Reeves, Sheri is having a difficult time at school. Before the accident, she was one of the top students in her class, but now, she is a changed child. Tommy and I get so anxious every time we get a call from her teacher because we know that we are probably going to hear some upsetting news about Sheri.

"Hmmm… it looks like you might want to think about moving her to a new school system," he said.

"What are you suggesting?" Tommy asked.

"I live on Mercer Island and am quite impressed with its school system, Dr. Reeves explained. I recently referred another family with a special needs child to the Mercer Island Elementary School and they are very happy with how their child has adjusted since she has been going there."

"Mercer Island? I asked. Isn't that a very wealthy community? My salon is in Seattle, but I have many clients who come from Mercer Island and they appear to be pretty well-off financially."

"Kay, put your feelings aside and think about what's best for Sheri," said Dr. Reeves, as he tried to reason with us.

Taking his advice to heart, we took a deep breath and invested in a modest one-level house that was located in the middle of Mercer Island. This community is conveniently located on Lake Washington between two large cities, Seattle and Bellevue, and is one of the most affluent enclaves in the area. We were immediately out of our comfort zone. After living there a while, it was obvious that the school was not well-suited for Sheri. We ended up bussing her east to the nearby Issaquah School District, where they had a special education class that could address her needs. Our son, Ross, who was three years younger and a shy child, didn't seem to enjoy his life on Mercer Island, either. We soon realized that Dr. Reeves meant well, but didn't really seem to know what was best for Sheri and the complex problems resulting from her head injury.

I tried to support the small businesses on Mercer Island and developed a close business relationship with Margaret, who owned a small hair salon on the island. Because it was conveniently located in the town center and pretty close to where we lived, I dropped by to visit fairly often. It was easy for me to visit on the way to work or on my way home from Pioneer Square. I liked the feel of her small, 1,000 square-foot salon and she always welcomed me with a cheerful smile when I walked in. Margaret was an attractive woman with long, dark brown hair who was always immaculately dressed from head to toe and had an air of confidence about her.

Meeting with Margaret about her business was always enjoyable because she was open to advice and listened intently when I presented her with new ideas. When she heard something that she liked, she threw all of her effort behind it to make things work. The big question in my mind was always whether she could make the switch from being a hair stylist to a professional business owner. I wondered whether she had the leadership skills to build a team out of her group of self-serving and independent stylists.

At one of my visits to her salon, I recommended that she remove the small televisions that were mounted on the walls of some of the cubicles. I said to her, "Margaret, I don't think the stylists and customers in your salon should be watching television. It's more important that the stylists give their undivided attention to each of their customers and provide a unique experience focused on what can be done to their hair and emotional well-being."

"Okay, I'll give it a try, but it will be hard, she tried to explain. "We're so used to watching television in the salon all day."

It was New Year's Eve. My staff and I were cleaning up after an extremely busy day of work. Everyone was anxious to leave so that they could celebrate this last day of the year with their friends and families.

Naomi, our front desk manager, suddenly appeared in the dispensary. "Kay, can you come over here? Margaret, the salon owner from Mercer Island, is on the phone. I think you'd better take this call. She sounds pretty upset."

I ran to the phone and said, "Hi Margaret. Are you all right?" I asked.

Margaret's voice was shaking as she said, "Kay, I can't take this any longer. I feel like I'm going to have a nervous breakdown. I am not cut out to be a business owner."

"Now Margaret, please get a hold of yourself. What happened? Why are you saying this?" I asked.

"*Everything* happened. I'm not able to handle my staff. I am too stressed out and I can't go on like this day in and day out. I need to preserve my health."

"Wow, hold on. I guarantee that you will feel differently tomorrow," I said, trying to reason with her.

"No, I won't," she explained. "I have decided that all I want to do now is to sell the salon and get out of the business."

"You don't mean that Margaret," I said, as I tried to reason with her. "You've been trying so hard to make things work."

"I am dead serious, Kay, she said. "I called because I wanted to ask you if you would consider buying my salon. If anyone can make a go of this salon, it's you."

I took a deep breath and said, "Margaret, let's talk more in a few weeks. You will be a lot calmer and will have had a chance to think things through before making such a big decision."

To make a long story short, I became the owner of a small Mercer Island salon for a buy-out fee of $90,000.

CHAPTER 27:

GETTING DOWN TO BUSINESS
ON THE ROCK

The first walkthrough in the small salon that I had just purchased was quite an eye-opener. The 1,000 square foot salon was located on 78th Avenue on Mercer Island (often referred to as "the Rock"), in a strip mall across from a fire station. The narrow entry to the salon had limited exposure to passersby, so you really had to look hard to find it.

On this first visit after Margaret's salon had closed its doors, I gingerly entered the quiet and empty space alone, walking through the narrow pathway that led to the styling stations. Each of the stations was enclosed in a cubicle with chest-high walls covered in wall paper. Small-screen televisions were suspended from the ceiling. My immediate reaction was a big "Ugh." The first thing I knew I had to do was to peel off the three layers of wallpaper. Flower prints were definitely not my favorite motif to look at on a daily basis.

I silently calculated the costs to make all the changes that would have to be completed before I could call it by the name I had chosen:

Studio 904 Mercer Island. To reflect the image that I wanted for my new salon, I felt I needed to gut the entire interior and start over. Unfortunately, I didn't have the funds to do a remodeling job of that magnitude. If I wanted to go down that path, I would have to re-mortgage my house again. The thought of adding more debt to my home scared me and I was quickly overwhelmed. I said to myself, "Kay, what were you thinking? You bought a beauty *parlor*, not a beauty *salon*. People on Mercer Island, especially the women, are not going to patronize a salon unless it looks like the same high-end boutiques that are in downtown Seattle." Unless my salon looked the part, potential customers would not be convinced that I could deliver the fashionable haircuts and colors they were used to getting. Realistically, I knew that I would have to do a miracle makeover on the staid, outdated décor if I was going to attract the customers I wanted. And I knew I had to do it without spending a ton of money.

The solution was to pull some money from my Pioneer Square salon and use it to remodel the new one. I felt comfortable doing that because the Pioneer Square salon had been steadily growing. It was profitable and stable, with a loyal client base that loved us. Fortunately, I was able to set aside re-mortgaging of my home for the time being. It already had a large, first mortgage attached to it, courtesy of the extra funds I previously needed to build out the now demolished Studio 904 salon on Pine Street.

With the help of my husband and a few friends, we rolled up our sleeves and worked together to take off layers of wallpaper, knock out the cubicle walls, remove the televisions, and splash on a coat of brilliant white paint to cover the multi-colored walls. The results were amazing! The salon looked brighter and larger with a clean, contemporary feel. There was a lot more that I wanted to do, but I decided to slowly fix things when I had the funds. I continually reminded myself to follow the Kaizen way of doing things - be patient, take one step at a time, and it will all work out.

The next thing on my "to do" list was to come up with a catchy message that I could send out to the Mercer Island community. I wanted to stress that Studio 904 was not just an ordinary neighborhood salon, but one with stylists who had artistic and technical skills that were worth trying. After putting a lot of thought into our marketing strategy, I came up with a slogan that I felt good about. I purchased a large display ad in the *Mercer Island Reporter*, the local newspaper. The ad's bold caption read: "THE WAIT IS OVER! STUDIO 904 BRINGS THE CITY TO MERCER ISLAND."

Our doors finally opened in August, 1998, just prior to the beginning of a new school year. I launched our first day of business by promoting a big fundraising event. We offered $10 haircuts for students, with the promise that all proceeds from the day would be donated to the Mercer Island Family and Youth Services organization. The money would be used to purchase backpacks and school supplies for children in low-income families. Our "Backpacks for Kids!" ad instantly drew the attention of mothers on Mercer Island and our appointment book was quickly filled.

The promotion was a big success; we had definitely found a popular way to give back to the community. Balloons decked the outside of our door, the salon was filled with the sounds of upbeat music, and the stylists and I wore black t-shirts with logos that read: "Many Cultures, One World."

A local media station sent a camera crew to the salon to film our event. I was elated when I saw coverage for our Backpack for Kids! promotion on the television news that evening!

What caught the parents' attention were three large gift baskets, each filled with hair products and a $50 Studio 904 gift certificate. The baskets were wrapped in clear cellophane paper tied with colorful ribbons. A large sign on the table told clients about our Backpack for Kids! program and asked parents to enter a raffle to win one of the baskets by filling out a ticket with their name, address, phone number, and e-mail address. It was hard to resist our offer and nearly everyone dropped a raffle ticket into the large glass bowl before they left.

At the end of the day, there were more than fifty raffle tickets in the glass bowl! As I reached into the bowl to draw the names of the three winners, I literally patted myself on the back, and thought, "Kay, this is the most important thing you could have done to put Studio 904 on the map in Mercer Island. You have fifty names and all sorts of contact information so you can now begin to market your unique services to the island's residents. More importantly, you contributed to the community and provided dozens of needy students with backpacks and school supplies."

One of the most important things that I did to grow our client base on Mercer Island was to send out regular newsletters with a familiar format. Each newsletter covered the following:

- Studio 904's philosophy of teamwork with non-commissioned stylists; honest, up-front pricing with a no-tipping policy; accurate record keeping; our money-back guarantee program; and our trained and skill-certified stylists.

- Updates on our various community service projects.

- Money-saving promotions for clients, such as Senior Prime Time for clients over 55; discounted times for teens and teachers; Men's Express times; and bonuses for referring new clients to Studio 904.

- A special story of the month that would be of interest to our clients.

Over time, customers were drawn in by our unique business

management approach and we won their trust by being an integral member of the community. We knew that we had won our customers' trust when they began referring their family members and friends to Studio 904. Even today, referrals of friends, family, and co-workers by satisfied customers remain our best source of new clients.

I think back to the beginning, when all of the naysayers said, "Kay, you aren't making a very good decision by opening a salon on Mercer Island. The residents there are not known for supporting locally-owned businesses. I would sure hate to see you fail." At this point in time, I was happy to prove them wrong because things were going extremely well.

Although the business was showing definite promise, it was not an easy journey to get to this point. There were numerous "hiccups" along the way that tested my patience and forced me to alter some of the ways I ran my salon.

I knew the stylists who worked for Margaret because of the staff training sessions I had provided for her salon. When she sold the business to me, each of her four stylists asked if they could continue working in the salon. I felt confident that they would be comfortable with my business philosophy because I had trained them on how to work in a non-commissioned, team environment and how to provide a high level of customer service. My confidence, however, was short-lived. What was I thinking? I should have known better than to assume that things would fall neatly into place.

For the first few weeks, I spent a lot of time driving on the I-90 floating bridge, going back and forth between my salons in Seattle and Mercer Island to train my twenty-four employees. I also occasionally spent time talking to customers from both salons because I had made my e-mail address and phone number readily available and encouraged clients to contact me if there were any questions or problems with the services they received at the salons.

My cell phone rang just as I was finishing up a styling class with a new hire in the Pioneer Square salon.

I answered, "This is Kay, how may I help you?"

With a hesitant voice, she said, "Hello Kay, my name is Gladys Schaffer, a customer in your Mercer Island salon."

"Oh, yes. Gladys, how may I help you?"

"Well, I don't usually complain, but I thought you would want to know about an incident that upset me last night while my two children were getting their haircuts."

"Yes, I certainly do want to know. Please tell me. What happened?" I asked, as my stomach felt like it was about to drop to the ground.

"I took my children to your salon to get their haircuts at around 7:00 p.m. and I was shocked at the behavior of two of your stylists, Rachel and Sam"

"Please, go on Gladys. Tell me exactly what happened," I said.

"They were exchanging lewd jokes while cutting my children's hair," she replied.

"What?" I asked, astonished.

"I couldn't believe what I was hearing. It angered me that that my children were being exposed to such crude talk. We won't be returning to your salon again and I want my money back."

"Yes, of course Gladys. We will certainly refund your money. I'm so sorry that this happened and I will make sure that such behavior never happens again," I said, apologizing profusely.

I was hurt, embarrassed, and humiliated, and could not believe that Margaret's former employees would act like this. There was no way that I could tolerate that kind of behavior in my salon. I immediately drove to the Mercer Island salon and terminated Rachel and Sam's employment. In the following week, I fired the other two stylists for displaying similarly rude and unprofessional behavior in the salon.

Now what was I going to do? Standing in my now empty Mercer Island salon, I tried to strategize my next move. I decided to seek out new stylists who were just graduating from cosmetology schools to hire and train. Unfortunately, they would not be ready to serve clients for at least six months because it would take hours of training for them to reach an acceptable competency level. In the meantime, how could I keep my doors open for business? There was only one answer. I would have to bring over three of my experienced stylists from the Pioneer Square salon. Because she had such excellent customer service skills, I also decided to ask Naomi, the front desk manager, to join the stylists. Naomi had something close to a photographic memory. She remembered the names of every client, as well as their detailed personal profiles. Everyone who came to Studio 904 immediately bonded with her. A typical client greeting went something like this: "Hello Mary, it's so nice to see you. Would you like your usual green tea with a spoonful of sugar? And how is your daughter, Amy, doing? I remember the last time you were here, you told me that she was chosen to represent her school on the debate team." Her customer service skills never ceased to amaze me. I was convinced that with the two of us working together, we could grow the Mercer Island salon's client base.

To make up for not having an adequate number of trained stylists, I also worked long hours as a stylist on the design floor, providing services to our customers for the next six months. With Naomi at the front desk and the experienced stylists from Pioneer Square, we were able to draw in new clients on Mercer Island and nurture their loyalty to our salon. I started to hear frequent, heartwarming remarks from people who came to the salon. "Kay, you have an amazing team here. Everyone is *so* friendly and helpful. And, I *love* my hair!"

Meanwhile, back at the Pioneer Square salon, things weren't quite as rosy. I had to hire a new front desk manager to replace Naomi as well as hire three new stylists. Revenues started dropping every month. The new stylists were eating up payroll dollars and were not producing any income for the salon because of their inexperience. Clients began to complain that their high expectations for our services were not being met. It felt like I was constantly trying to keep two ships afloat. I often struggled to make the payroll for both salons and was repeatedly rejected when I attempted to borrow more money from the bank to meet my overhead costs for both locations. Finally, I had no choice but to take out another mortgage on my home.

To make matters worse, my bookkeeper suddenly resigned. During one of our working sessions, Betty informed me about her decision to leave. "Kay, I'm giving you my notice to quit."

"What? You can't leave me now, I need you to help me during this tough time," I responded, bewildered.

"I can't do this job any more. The work is stressing me out."

"Oh no, please hang in here with me for just a little longer," I pleaded.

"Kay, I personally think that you should think about filing bankruptcy, she said, with a stern look on her face. You will have a difficult time getting out of this mess. Your rent in Mercer Island is way too high and you're still carrying debt from your old salon that was demolished. Do you know how many haircuts it takes every month to pay just your rent? You should ask the landlord here to help you out. Another problem is that your payroll is eating you alive! These stylists are getting trained on your dollar without bringing in the income that you need to pay them. The only way to survive is to go back to paying them on a commission basis; your only responsibility is to pay them if they perform services. Furthermore, if this was my salon, I would cut out all the personal benefits you are paying them. I've never heard of a hair salon that pays for vacation, sick days, and medical and dental insurance. Only large corporations can afford to cover all of those benefits."

I was devastated at what I was hearing. Betty named one thing after another that was wrong with my business and it was hard to take.

"Here's another thing you need to cut out," she continued. "Quit donating time and money to community organizations. You need the money more than they do. You need to help yourself first."

With all of that said, Betty promptly walked out of the office and I never saw her again.

At the time, I felt abandoned. I was literally between the proverbial "rock and a hard place," which seemed ironic because one of my businesses was on Mercer Island. "Perhaps Betty *was* right. Maybe I *did* need to file for bankruptcy. I fought that idea for a long time because I knew that I couldn't give up. What motivated me was that I was convinced that my business model was the appropriate one for the salon industry and for the world. Even if it meant working my fingers to the bone and eating tuna fish sandwiches for dinner, I needed to stay true to myself, my beliefs, and my values.

As far as giving back to the community, it never dawned on me to cut any of those efforts. It was part of my soul and just too important to me.

After thinking through my situation and getting encouragement from those around me, I decided to move forward. Even though I was "this close" to giving up, I was convinced that if a few things broke my way, I could make everything work and preserve my business. Sure, it was going to take some time to turn things around, but I believed that if I worked hard work and stuck to my principles, my vision for the business would be realized. When that day came, and I knew that it would, all of my efforts would be even more gratifying.

CHAPTER 28:

CREATING A COMPASSIONATE
WORKPLACE

When Mother brought me to the United States, I devoted most of my energy toward learning the English language. Entering school at the age of eleven and not knowing a word of English was difficult. Some of my classmates teased me relentlessly. I like to think that it was a case of "kids being kids," and having no clue as to how hurtful it was for me. If they understood the meaning of the words "empathy" and "compassion," I'm pretty sure they wouldn't have acted the way they did. Instead, they may have extended their hands to me in a gesture of friendship. With the diverse student populations in today's class-rooms, my spirits are lifted when I hear about efforts by teachers and schools to create environments in which differences are valued and respected, and empathy and compassion for others is encouraged.

I believe that having empathy – understanding and sharing the feelings of another – is the key to having a happy and fulfilling life, both personally and professionally. I wanted my stylists to have not only empathy with their clients, but also to show them compassion.

Having no idea how to teach these concepts to my stylists, I tried by continually reminding them, "Remember, we are giving our customers more than haircuts and styles. We are here to listen and to understand their emotional needs and to provide our services with empathy and compassion. You must learn the art of putting yourselves in their shoes."

As luck would have it, the perfect opportunity to illustrate my point happened to walk into the salon one day. Karlene, one of our regular clients, brought Helen, her elderly mother, in for a haircut. Helen was frail and I could see that she was unhappy. Concerned, I changed my schedule and decided to give her a haircut and style myself. I wanted to make sure that she was given the extra time and attention I thought she needed.

Before I started, Karlene quickly pulled me aside.

"I thought I should let you know that my mother was diagnosed with stomach cancer a month ago," she whispered. "She's going through chemotherapy now and it's been just awful. She's been horribly depressed and unhappy."

My heart clenched. "Oh, no! I am sorry to hear that and I understand how she must be feeling. I've gone through this sort of thing with some of my family members."

"I brought her in today because I thought that getting a nice haircut and style would lift her spirits," Karlene explained.

"I'll listen carefully to what she wants and make sure that she loves the final result," I promised. "Does your mother live with you?"

"No, she is very stubborn about her independence, Karlene replied. My mother had a very productive and successful life as a school teacher and still feels that she is capable of living on her own. I can see, however, that she is having a difficult time with loneliness and isolation. The majority of her friends have passed on, so she doesn't really have anyone to socialize with now."

I thanked Karlene for being so forthcoming and slowly approached her mother. As I began to cut and style Helen's hair, I made sure to keep her engaged in making decisions about her haircut and style. I also asked her about her experiences as a school teacher, while my scissors snipped away at her thinning hair. Despite her depression, she was easy to talk to and, at times, even humorous.

After the last finishing touches, I handed Helen a small mirror and turned her chair around slowly so she could see herself from all angles. She was thrilled!

"Wow! Is this me?" she gasped.

I beamed at her while looking at the mirror.

"Oh my, I didn't think I could look this good. I've looked like a rat lately, haven't I?" she said to her daughter.

Karlene walked over and gave her mother a gentle hug. I was touched to see tears welling up in her eyes, a telling sign of how much her mother's happiness meant to her.

"I wish I could look like this every day," added Helen. "It would be such a nice distraction from the rest of this misery I am going through."

I immediately saw an opportunity to help Helen and Karlene and, at the same time, provide my stylists with an example of what I meant when I reminded them to pay attention to their clients' emotional needs. As they were leaving the salon, I caught up with Helen and Karlene.

"Helen, would you be open to coming to our salon again?" I asked. "We would be happy to give you a relaxing shampoo and style your hair so that every day you will look just as beautiful as you do today."

"Oh, I would like that very much!" she replied, excitedly.

"But, I don't think my mother can afford such a luxury more than once every few months," Karlene hedged.

"You won't have to worry about that, I said. "I'm proposing that she comes in to have her hair done every week. Miya will be assigned as her personal stylist and it won't cost you a cent."

"What? You're willing to do this for free?" Karlene replied, incredulously.

"Completely. There won't be any charge," I happily confirmed.

I knew this was the right thing to do. Helen's big, appreciative smile was all the confirmation I needed

Before long, all of my staff was involved in Helen's weekly Tuesday morning visits to Studio 904. Miya was her assigned stylist, but everyone helped out to give her the most welcoming and comforting services possible during every visit to the salon.

Some days, Helen came in looking upset and in noticeable pain, so we did everything we could to lift her spirits. We gave her soothing shampoos combined with head and neck massages. When we had time, one of the stylists would give her a hand massage with our favorite hand cream. We did our best to make her laugh, but, most of all, we listened to the fascinating stories that she told us from her years of teaching special education.

Each time we finished, Helen would smile at herself in the mirror and exclaim, "Wow, you did it again. I look so beautiful!"

One Tuesday morning, Helen failed to show up for her regular appointment and everyone in the salon was concerned. We received a call from Karlene that afternoon, informing us that her mother had passed away earlier that morning. A few days later, a beautiful bouquet of pink and white flowers was delivered to our front desk. The attached note read: "I want you all to know how much happiness you brought to me in my last days on this earth...more than you can ever imagine. Thank you. With all my love, Helen."

There wasn't a dry eye in the salon as we read this deeply touching note in Helen's own handwriting. I silently thanked the wonderful lady for teaching all of us the real meaning empathy and compassion.

CHAPTER 29:

ONE STEP AT A TIME, WITH A STOMACH MADE OF IRON

Throughout the years, I scrimped and saved and worked long hours to build my business. I thought about it 24 hours a day, but often felt like I was not succeeding at a fast-enough pace. For me, every year seemed like a financial struggle. I looked around at my peers who owned small businesses and saw them driving fancy cars and traveling all over the world to attend exciting business symposiums. It wasn't unusual to hear them talking about their trips to places like Greece, Paris, London, or Tokyo.

"What am I doing wrong?" I wondered. Why was I seemingly behind the other business owners? What was missing in my management skills? I often felt hopeless and discouraged.

When I needed encouragement, my mind often drifted back to Aesop's classic story of *The Tortoise and the Hare*, which was one of my favorite books to read as a child. As I thought about my business, the Tortoise reminded me of business owners like myself who were slow and steady, but always aiming toward a goal. The Hare remind-ed me of the business owners I met who seemed to be constantly sprinting, but didn't have their eyes fixed on a specific objective.

This story kept me motivated enough to push forward, but it did little to help me deal with the stark realities of running my own busi-ness. At social gatherings, people asked, "How is your business do-ing? You're making a lot of money, right?" I didn't know how to re-ply to such questions and wondered if I should tell them the truth and say, "I've been eating tuna fish sandwiches for dinner every night so that I could cover my payroll last week."

"Oh, business is going good," I always replied. I certainly didn't want to come across as a down-and-out business owner.

In truth, I wanted to scream, "Do you know how hard it is to make payroll every week? What about my monthly expenses and tax-es?" But I felt very alone as a struggling, small business owner.

Before I started my business, I had heard people say that own-ing your own business puts you on the road to wealth and happiness. What could be better than being your own boss? Now, I wasn't sure if this was a myth or if I was doing something wrong.

I really didn't know what to say when my peers said, "You're so lucky that you can deduct all of your business expenses and pay less in taxes. With what you save, you can afford to travel or buy a new car."

Maybe it's because I had too much pride that I didn't object and explain to them that any potential tax benefits paled in comparison with my actual business expenses.

One day, I walked one of my clients, Meredith, up to the front desk after styling her hair. I picked up one of our Studio 904 promotional brochures and gave it to her. She looked at the inside cover and exclaimed, "Oh, you believe in the Kaizen philosophy! I work for a hospital and we're using the same thing to improve our systems and customer service."

"Yes," I said, "I was born in Japan and the concept of lifelong learning in small, incremental steps was something that I heard about when I was growing up."

"I can certainly tell that you are now learning to practice the art of Kaizen at Studio 904. Keep believing in it and follow the Kaizen principles every day. You will eventually end up in the right place," she said.

Taking her advice to heart, I became more focused on making small steps forward instead of comparing myself with other business owners and trying to live up to other people's expectations. Every morning when I woke up, I would say to myself, *"take small incremental steps, one at a time."* I have tried to maintain this ritual for the past several years. Reciting the reminder each day is easy, but putting it into practice on a regular basis is sometimes a struggle.

One year, I attended a conference sponsored by the Small Business Administration. I sat in a room with 40 local business owners and listened to presentations on topics such as human resources, marketing, and finance. The shock for me came at the end of the presentation on finances. The instructor pointed to the four corners of the room and said, "Now, I want to see how many years each of you has been in business. Please go to your area as I call out the years."

I wondered what he was trying to prove. I didn't like being singled out and felt very nervous.

"Everyone, please listen carefully. Everyone who has been in business for three years or less, please move to this corner of the room," he said.

Around 70% of the people moved to the corner of the room he pointed to.

He continued, "How many of you have been in business for three-to-seven years?" A hand-full of participants moved to their designated corner.

"All of the people who have been in business for seven-to-twelve years, go to that corner," the instructor instructed. Only two people went to that corner. By this time, I was the only one not standing in a corner.

"The last corner is for people who have been in business for 18 years or longer. I see that only one person is left," he said as he looked at me, "So how many years have you been in business?"

I was a bit self-conscious, but said, "I've been in business for 28 years."

"Wow, that is a record-breaker!" the instructor exclaimed.

"Everyone, please give this woman a big round of applause. She is a survivor!"

I must have looked stunned, as the whole room clapped. People came up to me wanting to know my secrets for longevity in the business world.

That moment was when I realized that there are no winners in small businesses; there are only survivors. Many of the trendy, small business owners whom I had envied in the past, had gone by the wayside. And yet, here I was, still standing.

Now, when people tell me I'm successful, I always reply with, "I don't know if I consider myself successful, but I know for sure that I AM A SURVIVOR."

CHAPTER 30:

THE PERFECT TURNKEY BUSINESS

One day, I noticed a client, someone whom I had never seen before. She was walking up to the front desk to pay for her haircut. Before she had a chance to leave, I ran up to her to introduce myself and to thank her for visiting my salon. She surprised me by exclaiming, "So, this is your salon? I *love* how my hair turned out, but I *really love* your friendly staff and the organic feel of your salon!"

"Oh, what exactly do you mean?" I asked, inquisitively.

"I love how your salon is decorated using natural fabrics. I even made a comment to your stylist who cut my hair. She told me that you personally made all of the darling, white "Owl Angels" by painting brown, paper grocery bags, stuffing them, and then decorating the bags with lace. After that, she explained how you maintained the aesthetics of the salon by displaying new decorations every season to complement all of your community service projects."

"Yes, I do all of those things," I replied, proudly. "I love to see the delight in our customers' faces when they come in and see that our salon is decorated to reflect the different seasons of the year as well as the various holidays. Life is often tough for all of us. With so many disappointing and unexpected events, I want to provide an environment that promotes a whimsical and uplifting energy when customers visit the salon."

"You're not only an entrepreneur, but a talented artist, too!" she exclaimed.

"Thank you so much for noticing. I hope to see you when you come back for your next hair service," I replied.

"Oh, I will *definitely* be back! This is a *very* special salon," she said, as she smiled and walked toward the door.

Comments like this made all the difference in the world to me. From the beginning, my goal was to attract the "right" kind of employees to my business. Additionally, it was important for me to regularly interact with customers who shared my values - people who had caring hearts and enthusiasm to live life to its fullest.

Some of the best and busiest times to be in the salon are during our weekly promotions. "Senior Prime Time" is dedicated to clients who are fifty-five years or older and we also have promotions when we discount services for particular groups of clients, like a "Men's Express" day and a "Student/Teacher" day. I love to be in the salon on those days because everyone seems to be happy and the salon is buzzing with activity. During moments like these, it feels like my vision for the salon has become a reality.

Meanwhile, in my personal life, friends who saw me working tirelessly day after day, would often say, "You spend a lot of your time training stylists. Don't you ever get tired of teaching and training? You must not have any time to do anything else."

My automatic response was, "Yes, sometimes. I work so hard because I want our customers to have the best-skilled stylists and our undivided attention when they come to Studio 904. One weak link on our team will ruin everything that I am striving for. I have to make sure that every team member is just as good as the next, so that we never disappoint a single customer."

In return, they would often respond, "But many of your stylists seem to work for you just to get trained. After that, they leave when they think they've learned enough to go out on their own. That must make you feel kind of angry after putting in that much time and effort."

"I never know what anyone's intentions are when they come to work at the salon, but it's important that I properly train each person," I would explain. "The worst scenario for our customers is to have untrained stylists. If that happens, I may as well shut my doors."

Nodding their heads, they would often commiserate and say, "It's a good thing that you have such a positive attitude. I am not sure that I would have the patience to do all of that."

"I really don't see my training efforts as being wasted," I would conclude. I feel good that everyone who leaves Studio 904 is going out into the world with more knowledge than they had before they came to work for me. They may not think about it at the time, but I'm sure that one day they will realize how much they learned here, not only as far as the technical skills they acquired, but also the understanding of what it takes to become a better human being."

Could this be true? I picked up the local newspaper, the *Mercer Island Reporter*, one morning to check on the latest community news when I saw a headline that read, "Studio 904 has been chosen as the *"The Best Salon to Get Your Haircut!"* The article listed all of the ways that our salon had contributed to making Mercer Island a great place to live and it also provided a number of glowing endorsements from some of our clients. "Wow, this is too good to be true," I thought. To top it off, we also subsequently received a "Philanthropy Award" from the Mercer Island Family and Youth Services organization for our contributions to families in need.

With that kind of positive press and free word-of-mouth advertising, we quickly outgrew the small, 1,000 square foot salon that I purchased from Margaret. No matter how tough things got, I kept up with my monthly payments and the salon was soon paid off in full. To accommodate the increase in clients, I decided to negotiate a new lease with the landlord and build a larger salon with a total of 2,400 square feet of space in the same building complex. Comparing the cost of my former lease with the new one was pretty terrifying. I felt good about my decision, though, because the extra room would provide a more open salon environment, which I desperately wanted. In addition, there would be more space for community fundraisers and educational forums. By offering a place to gather, to educate, and to nurture one's soul, I could provide opportunities to generate uplifting experiences, as well as fulfill my vision of lifelong learning. The additional space would also allow me to hold special arts and crafts classes for those who showed an interest in learning how to make the decorations they saw in the salon throughout the year. It was fun to see the participants' creative juices rise to the surface. Many of them squealed with delight when they saw the results of the beautiful handmade cards and objects they created. A comment that was often heard went something like this, "I never dreamed that I could create such a beautiful work of art. Projects like this are so great because I thought I didn't have an artistic bone in my body."

I have always enjoyed teaching people how to make things using their hands. A certain magic seems to happen when people work with colorful pieces of paper and fabrics. Because they are in a safe and comfortable environment, participants willingly share their life stories, often relating painful and joyous experiences to their new-found friends. Many friendships and close connections blossomed during these art classes as well as during fundraising events that I held in the salon. I have always felt strongly that there is a need for this kind of bonding as we all experience lives that are too often dictated by our busy schedules and multiple responsibilities.

It made me feel good to see that both of my salons were now running on solid ground. The quality assurance procedures I developed were all finally documented in Studio 904's *Operations Manual* and the *Book of Kaizen Employee Training Manual*. What felt even better was that the procedures were being followed by all of my employees. Watching the content of what I created being acted out in the salon was like watching an almost perfect play being performed every day. And, I was finally starting to pay off my accumulated debts every month. I had amassed a fairly large deficit due to the unfortunate events surrounding my first two salons. Subsequent financial obligations were also incurred because of a bad economy and frequent staff turnovers. As a result, working with a tight cash-flow became a way of life. Kaoru, my financial manager, and I worked hard to streamline our spending on a regular basis. Our motto was, "Penny saved, penny earned." Thankfully, having to exercise this kind of discipline in managing the salon's finances also helped me to become a better money manager in my personal life. I learned to save for the future in small, incremental amounts, even when things were tight. It was actually fun to watch as my savings grew each month.

Looking from the outside in, I'm sure that people watching the operations of Studio 904 got the impression that we were making tons of money. Clients and friends would often say, "Kay, it looks like your business is doing so well. It's always so busy whenever I come in. You're on your way to "Easy Street." You can finally afford to sit back and relax now." Deep down, however, I knew that relaxing was definitely not an option. There were always future trends to watch for and new technologies to keep up with. To stop growing because I felt like I was "out of the woods" would mean that I would be going backwards.

I think that people who run a small business truly understand that money is always tight. It is extremely difficult to make a profit after taking care of the payroll, inventory expenses, rent, and the high taxes that the government and city impose on small businesses. I knew two women who owned nearby businesses. One owned a flower shop and the other a dress boutique, but they never appeared to be very busy. When I asked them how they were able to survive, they mentioned that their families needed a tax write-off, so it was perfectly acceptable that their businesses didn't break even at the end of the year. Both of them closed their businesses in less than five years. They both said that all the hard work they had to put into the business wasn't worth it. I personally didn't want to go down that road because I knew that my results were definitely worth all of the time and money I was putting into the salons.

After several years of plugging away, it was rewarding to hear many of my peers in the business community, as well as consultants and experts, finally acknowledge my efforts. One person told me, "Kay, you've created the perfect model for a turnkey business. Anyone can step into one of your salons, unlock the doors, and run it smoothly with the systems you've put in place. It will make money without you being there. You've created a franchise model. It's time for you to open more salons and grow your business."

For the next year, I did my due-diligence with regard to how franchising programs worked so that I could make a good decision. I learned these important facts:

- By having multiple locations and drawing from surrounding communities, a service business can be very profitable.

- The recommended avenue to raise capital for this kind of growth is to seek outside investors to be involved in your business.

- There are complex laws that must be followed by the franchisor and franchisee in order to operate a successful franchise empire.

- Many lawsuits have been filed due to some of the ambiguous business policies laid out in the contracts.

The idea of expanding beyond my two salons, Studio 904 Pioneer Square, and Studio 904 Mercer Island, sounded like an exciting option for me to explore. I knew I was at a critical crossroads in my career. However, before I could think about the future direction I wanted my business efforts to take, I felt I needed to spend the time to consider what was truly important to me. It was time once again to go to the top of the mountain to do some deep soul-searching about myself and to seek additional advice from my most trusted advisor.

CHAPTER 31:

GROW YOUR OWN ROSE GARDEN

I sat across from Joe, my devoted mentor. We were in a quiet and pleasant restaurant located in an upscale, retirement facility near my salon on Mercer Island. It was one of our favorite places to meet because we were able to have a leisurely lunch. Unlike other restaurants, the staff never asked us to hurry our meal so that they could seat other guests. As a person who always led by example, Joe insisted on conducting our lunch meetings in either moderately-priced or inexpensive restaurants.

"Mmmm... this is excellent soup, don't you think?" he said, as he sipped his first spoonful of steaming hot, chicken noodle soup.

"Yes, it is *very* good," I agreed.

"Kay, I can tell that something serious is on your mind today. Am I right? Is everything going well with your business?" he asked.

"Yes, Joe. Everything is going extremely well in the salon," I replied.

"Last time we met, you had so many glowing reports to give me, but you have hardly had anything to say today. After reviewing some of your reports before this meeting, however, I did notice that your financials are now showing a remarkable improvement in terms of reducing your debt load. Good job, Kay."

After pausing for a minute, I said, "Actually, Joe, I do have something very important to discuss with you today and I really need your advice." After the words came out of my mouth, Joe's reassuring smile again gave me the comfort I needed to reveal a few things that I could never discuss with anyone else. Perhaps it was because he was just as concerned about my personal well-being as my business. When I wanted to make personal sacrifices to keep the business going, he consistently told me that taking care of my personal security and happiness should be the first priority.

Continuing on, I said, "I think I've reached a crossroads in my life and career. A lot of people have approached me lately and told me that they think I have created the ideal "turnkey" business to grow my business beyond the locations in Pioneer Square and Mercer Island."

"Kay, you've certainly worked hard to create a business plan with a solid foundation. I'm impressed with the step-by-step details you've documented in your human resources, marketing, and operations manuals. Your *Book of Kaizen Training Manual* for new hires surpasses anything I've seen," he said. "In addition, you've made your business transparent to your employees and you've put so much energy into training your employees to take on leadership roles." Joe concluded, "Kay, I believe your business will now run smoothly without you being there every day."

I nodded in agreement, feeling honored that Joe had such a high opinion of what I had created. It made me wonder, though, if he was telling me what he really felt or if he was simply trying to build up my ego so I'd feel more confident about expanding my businesses from two locations to potentially several more. He went on by saying, "But before we talk about expansion, I think you need to be very clear in your own mind about answers to some very big questions. The big questions I have for you are, "What are your ultimate goals in life going forward? What do you see yourself doing in the next two years, five years, and beyond that? What does a truly happy life look like to you?"

I could sense that he wasn't trying to steer me in one direction or another with regard to expanding the number of my salons. Although I was hoping that he would give me a black-and-white answer, I should have known better. As usual, he was being a good listener and asking thought-provoking questions in order to help me come up with the answer on my own.

"Kay, I jotted some more questions you might want to ask yourself between now and the next time we meet," he said.

I thought, "Oh, no. Now he's giving me some homework to do. I don't have time to do homework!" I tried not to show my annoyance by quickly replying, "Okay, I will work on it, Joe." However, what I really wanted to say to him was, "Can you help me come up with the answers?"

He must have read my mind because he quickly came back and said, "Oh, by the way, Kay, I recommend that you don't take any more classes, read any more business books, or seek out other people to give you the answers. I think it is time that you write your own book and start teaching people all that you know. Even though you may not think so, you have a great deal of practical knowledge from your years of experience in building a successful business. You are in a great position to train fledgling entrepreneurs and save them from the same heartaches that you have experienced."

We said our goodbyes with a warm hug and then he walked toward his car. At that moment, I had the feeling that I could conquer anything that I wanted to take on. It was one of the priceless things that Joe instilled in me every time we met.

As he suggested, I spent the next three months focusing on finding the answers to what I really liked doing and what I didn't particular care to do. I concentrated on creating a vision about how I wanted to see myself in the years to come and became acutely aware of my personal feelings as I lived every moment of my day-to-day schedule.

Randi, a friend of mine, recently retired from her government job, and now spent every day playing golf. She would frequently say to me, "I love playing golf and wish that you would take some time to start smelling the roses, too. I know that you would love the life of leisure that I am now living." When she made these comments, I never knew what to say, but usually responded with an agreeable answer, such as "Yes, one day I'll be able to enjoy myself playing golf, just like you."

"I don't think that will happen until you sell your salons and get out of the business completely," she always replied.

"That would be too hard for me to do because I love my work," was my typical response.

"Well, I have to admit, of all of my friends, I have never heard anyone who thinks and talks like you when it comes to their work," she would concede.

To get more focused on what I wanted to do and where I wanted to go in the next several years, I picked up a piece of paper and scribbled down Joe's questions, followed by my answers:

What don't you like doing?

- Driving back and forth from my Mercer Island salon to the Pioneer Square salon makes me anxious. Because so much time is spent traveling on the road, I never feel like I have the time to make a positive impact on either salon. I don't like being torn between two salons because I love both of them. I continually ask myself, "Where do I *really* belong?"

- I don't enjoy the constant money problems and trying to balance out the weekly sales at the two salons. It always feels like I am on a teeter totter; when one end is up, the other end is down. I worry about my sales revenue twenty-four hours a day. It is a constant battle to stay afloat.

- I don't like to borrow money from banks. Actually, I feel uncomfortable asking *anyone* for money. Targeting investors to fund any type of business expansion would not come naturally to me.

What do you like doing?

- I like having the time to personally interact with our customers and find solutions to their unique hair and style challenges. Helping clients find the right haircut and color is enjoyable for me. With my many years of experience, it is second nature. I know people's head shapes, hair textures, and physiques so well that my hands move naturally towards creating results that customers are elated with. This is the one thing I miss doing because I have to spend so much time training my employees.

- I want to live a "purpose-driven" life and make personal connections with children, animals, and volunteers who have the compassion to extend a helping hand to those in need. My philanthropic work is a passion of mine, and I want to do more in that area.

- I have other non-work-related dreams that I want to accomplish in my life, such as writing and publishing a book about my childhood and my unique journey in the business world. In addition, I want time to expand my love for art and make things with my hands.

What would an ideal life look like to me?

I love running my business, but I want to do it in a more focused way. If I developed my Mercer Island salon into a "destination business" that would attract customers from all over the area, I would not have to open salons in other communities to attract more customers. For this to work, I would need to learn and grow as an individual.

As I thought about this new direction in my personal and business life, I felt excitement and passion to move forward with my plan. After I completed my homework assignment, I picked up the phone and called Joe.

"Hello Kay, how are you?" he answered.

"Joe, I have some good news," I said excitedly.

"I'm ready to hear it. What did you want to tell me?" he asked.

"I completed the homework that you gave me and, believe it or not, I honestly answered all of the questions you asked," I said.

"Good. I am glad you approached the task so seriously. So, what did you decide to do?" he asked.

"I've decided *not* to expand my business into more locations. Instead, I have decided to downsize, concentrate on managing only one salon, and converting it into a really successful destination business. My customers will come from all over the Seattle area to one location instead of traveling to Studio 904 salons in different locations."

"That's great Kay, how are you planning to do that?" he asked.

"I'm going to sell my Pioneer Square salon!" I exclaimed.

Earlier, when my friend asked me when I was going to "smell the roses," I didn't have a sincere answer. Now, I do. The next time she asks, I will tell her and everyone else, "I *have* found my rose. Not only that, but I am cultivating an entire garden with beautiful roses of all colors and varieties that will grow all year long!"

WATCH MY VIDEO:

Chapter 31: Thank you and Lasting Words

http://keikokayhirai.com/chapter-31-thank-you-and-lasting-words/

LESSONS I LIVE BY

My journey has not only been a long one, but it has also been full of challenges and personal growth. When I felt like there was little hope, a window of opportunity often opened, providing me with new insights that exposed me to different perspectives and ways of thinking. I like to call these my "aha" moments – times when a fresh breeze made its way through my open window. Here are a few of the lessons I learned on my journey.

1 ✄ STRIVE FOR PEACEFUL RECONCILIATIONS BY STRENGTHENING OR MENDING RELATIONSHIPS.

Sometimes, we purposely part ways with people in our lives - often over some kind of conflict. At the time, it seems impossible to come to a peaceful parting because of the circumstances involved. It would be easy to quickly dismiss these people, but don't take that course of action. Continue to reach out to them no matter how long it takes. One day, you will find a reason to make a connection with them again.

When I published my book, *Yumi's Life Lessons*, I sent a copy to some of my ex-employees who had not departed on the best of terms. I enclosed a short note. Afterwards, I received phone calls from each one of them thanking me for the kind gesture. After all, how could they remain disgruntled when they had received a heartwarming book about a dog teaching you how to have a happy life? I created a list of steps that I have taken to make peaceful reconciliations.

> # DOWNLOAD:
> ## 12 Small Steps for Developing Strong Relationships
> http://keikokayhirai.com/smallsteps

2 YOU CAN'T DRAG PEOPLE TO THE TOP — THE DESIRE AND EFFORT TO EXCEL HAS TO COME FROM WITHIN EACH PERSON.

For years, I tried to push people to improve their skills and increase their capacity to think in creative and unconventional ways. I was often disappointed and frustrated when people did not live up to my expectations. Eventually, I came to understand that it was not up to *me* to drag people to the top. I realized that my energy is better spent as a teacher and mentor, and being a good listener.

Timing is also important as it may take multiple experiences and encounters with many different people to positively impact a person's life. I am always humbled and happy when one of my past employees drops by the salon and says, "Thank you. I learned a lot from you. At the time, I didn't appreciate it, but now I realize I've come this far in life because of you." These expressions of gratitude reinforce for me that teaching and mentoring are well worth my time and commitment.

3 ✄ CONTROL YOUR STRESS BY IGNORING THE SMALL STUFF AND FOCUSING ON THE BIG PICTURE.

A lot of people get stressed out because they focus on insignificant things that happen to their businesses or take place in their personal lives. A friend of mine, for example, got upset because she paid full price for a computer when she could have waited and bought it on sale. The result would have meant a savings of $150. I asked her, "Would you be any richer ten years from now because you saved $150 on your computer today?" After contemplating my question, I noticed that her stress immediately subsided when she realized that she was taking things a little too seriously.

4 ✄ BE A LIFELONG LEARNER - WHAT YOU KNOW TODAY IS NOT ENOUGH TO KEEP YOU ON TOP OF THIS FAST-MOVING WORLD.

What are you doing on a daily basis to keep your business viable or your personal life on the upward swing for the next several years? Recently, I reminded myself how fast things can change by taking a bottle of shampoo from our product display shelf. I thought, "This bottle of shampoo will be 24 hours older by tomorrow. A year from now, it may look entirely different or it may not even exist." I also regularly ask myself, "Do I know enough today to keep on top of this fast-moving world?" As a business owner, I know that I have to remain current so that I can keep my salon at the forefront of our competitive industry.

5 ✂ ATTITUDE IS EVERYTHING, SO SEE THE WORLD AND ITS EVENTS FROM A POSITIVE POINT OF VIEW.

Our society often places too much emphasis on talent to determine whether a person succeeds in their life and career. I couldn't disagree more. I've employed many people who had a natural talent for cutting and designing hair, plus an outgoing personality that appealed to clients. In the end, many of them were a disappointment and often left the salon after only a few months. In contrast, I have trained stylists who started out with only a minimal amount of creative flair for hair design, but had a passion for what they were doing, stuck it out for the long term, and won our clients' hearts. What was the one thing this latter group of stylists had in common? The answer is they approached life with a positive attitude.

6 ✂ EVERYONE HAS A GIFT THAT REVEALS ITSELF WHEN THEIR VALUES, PASSIONS, AND STRENGTHS MEET.

I believe that our willingness to use our unique personal gifts to bring about constructive societal change is a core attribute in all human beings. Living a purpose-driven life unleashes passion and love. My dream is that every human being will find his or her own distinctive gift and use it to make a positive difference in the world. I have served on many corporate boards and community organizing projects and observed many leaders in action. Some leaders were effective and others were not. I wondered what made the difference and came to the conclusion that good leaders help others discover their personal gifts and guide them on a path to put those gifts to good use.

> # DOWNLOAD:
> ## How to Find your Hidden Gifts
> http://keikokayhirai.com/hiddengifts

7 ✂ CREATE MAGICAL MOMENTS EVERY DAY BY GIVING PEOPLE MORE THAN THEY EXPECT.

A magical moment is a special feeling that one experiences; it could be very simple or something significant. What matters most, however, is that the special feeling brings delight and joy to your senses and you are inspired to move forward in a more positive direction. It doesn't take much. Here are some examples:

- Reach out to a stranger, give more of yourself to others, empathize with someone who needs it – all while trying to give them more than they expect. Surprise them!

- Be the first to smile and give a cheerful "Hello" to people you pass on your morning walk.

- Make everyday encounters special. Decorate your surroundings, serve your community, and create a pleasant environment everywhere you go!

- Keep your commitments. Show up when you say you will and stand up for causes that are important to you.

8 ✂ GOODBYES ARE HARD, BUT RECOGNIZE THAT THE ONLY CERTAINTY IN LIFE IS CHANGE.

If I had accepted early on that no one would be in my life forever, I would have saved myself a lot of heartache throughout the years. I used to put too much faith in people when I hired them to work in the salon or when I met people in special interest groups. After I gave them a lot of my energy and time, I felt a sense of sadness and betrayal when they went out of my life. Here is a valuable piece of advice I learned: Everyone is traveling through life on their own journey. It is only when two roads meet and align that two people actually walk the road together. That road will inevitably part at some point in time when each person chooses a different direction toward their next destination. Put in those terms, I am now able to handle my employees' departures with greater understanding.

9 ✂ CREATE SOMETHING NEW EVERY DAY.

I always carve out a short amount of time in each day to make something using my hands. The process of focusing your mind and soul and transforming simple objects into a beautiful piece of finished art brings out feelings of elation and satisfaction and gives me a new perspective on life. One of my favorite things to do is to take a brown grocery bag, cut it into various shapes, paint them with beautiful colors, and transform them into whimsical ornaments. I use these handmade ornaments to decorate my salon and create an up-lifting mood for our clients or sell them to raise money for my favorite charities. What can you make?

10 ✂ BUILD COMMUNITIES — THERE IS NOTHING MORE REWARDING THAN BRINGING DIVERSE GROUPS OF PEOPLE TOGETHER TO WORK TOWARD A COMMON CAUSE.

I once met a consultant who told me that he could help me make $1 million dollars in a year if I contracted with him to use his service.

When I didn't respond right away, he asked, "Kay, what would you do if you had $1 million in your hands right now?" I said, "I would expand my philanthropic and community building programs." Lost for words, he said, "You mean, you would give your money away to other people?" He was simply beside himself.

Thinking back to that day, I don't think he understood the deeper, underlying message that I was trying to tell him. What I should have said was this: "There is something that happens when you gather volunteers to help with a community service project. Giving money to help those in need is not the only reason for philanthropic acts. Just as heartwarming are the relationships created through the camaraderie of working together with like-minded people to lend a helping hand to people who need it."

Here's an example of what I did: In 2011, Japan's Tohoku area was hit by a devastating tsunami, resulting in the loss of thousands of lives. I gathered together a few friends and asked them if they would help me make hand-designed cards that would be sold with the proceeds going to help the people of Tohoku. They all responded "Yes!" As people heard about my card project, my salon's back room was filled with volunteers who organized themselves in teams. These teams came to the salon, formed a production line, and produced 1,000 cards. For me, one of the rewarding parts of the process was listening to the life stories shared by each of the volunteers as they created their cards. The youngest person in this group was 11 and the oldest was 82. The group was diverse and included senior citizens, young adults, people with disabilities, and people of color. Each brought snacks to share, while they laughed and cried as they made the cards. What was the end result? We raised $10,000 - sending $9,000 to the people of Tohoku and donating $1,000 to those who were caring for the homeless animals that were left behind by their owners. This fundraiser was one of the most beautiful and heartwarming projects that I have ever done.

11 ✂ CELEBRATE YOUR LIFE BY SHARING YOUR STORY.

Our life stories are unique to each one of us. When you open yourself to sharing a story, it not only heals your soul, but it also causes other people to return the gesture. After I wrote my memoir, *"Keiko's Journey,"* I was surprised at the healing effect it had. Sorting through everything in my head and finding the courage to share my life story with others impacted people far and wide. I felt like it was all worth it when people came up to me and said, "When I read your story, it brought back my own memories that I've kept inside of me for many years. Now, I have the courage to face them head on." Our personal stories are the glue that binds together who we are and what we have become. I encourage you to carve out little segments of your day to write about your past, your present, and your future.

Do you want to write your memoir? Check out the simple help guide I have created to get you started.

DOWNLOAD:
12 Steps for Writing Your Memoir (and why you should do it)
http://keikokayhirai.com/12steps

---

12 ✂ HELP YOURSELF BY PAYING IT FORWARD.

The often-heard phrase of "Paying It Forward" is a reminder to do something good as we live our lives each day. You perform a random act of kindness without expecting or hoping for anything in return from the person you are helping. What I have noticed, however, is that while we will pay an act of kindness forward with people we don't know, we don't always do the same for ourselves. I am amazed, for example, that only a small group of our customers take advantage of our Customer Loyalty gift cards that we sell. The cards offer an attractive discount; the higher the price of the card, the higher the discount received. I admire customers who manage their money so well that they can afford to pay a lump sum of $1,000 or more to take care of their personal hair needs one year in advance. So, in addition to paying it forward for strangers, try paying it forward for yourself. We all deserve a little kindness in our lives to brighten up our days!

13 ✂ WHEN YOU PERSEVERE, YOU CAN MAKE GOOD THINGS HAPPEN.

Here is my story: I felt helpless and frustrated when young single mothers, immigrant women, people on welfare, and high school graduates came to me, seeking a job. They couldn't afford the high tuition to enter a cosmetology school and many couldn't afford to stop working at their regular jobs for over a year to participate in the program.

While serving on the Governor's Small Business Improvement Committee, I came across an innovative training system called the Apprenticeship Program.

This program, if it was approved by the legislature, would be the first in our state for the cosmetology industry. "Kay, you have a well-established training program. You can become your own school and help people get their state cosmetology licenses while they learn on-the-job and earn a salary," said Jim from the Department of Labor and Industries.

With his encouragement, I recruited a group of salon owners to support a cosmetology apprenticeship program. I made regular trips to the state capitol in Olympia to meet with legislators to gain their support for the apprenticeship program. Aside from the constant and subtle intimidation I endured, I learned all about the state's political system - especially how a bill gets scrutinized from its introduction to its final passage by all political groups.

After eight years of hard work, my bill, titled "The Washington State Cosmetology Apprenticeship Program," finally passed into law in 2007. As I look back, I still can't believe that a single person, let alone me, could be the impetus for a major change in future state-supported training programs.

I share this story to provide hope to those who are feeling powerless to make a change in federal, state, or local governments. Remember. It doesn't take an army of people - just concerned citizens who are motivated to do what they believe is the right thing.

"Never doubt that a small group of thoughtful committed citizens can change the world; indeed, that's the only thing that ever has."

— Margaret Mead

14 ✄ GIVE WITH YOUR HEART TO HELP SOMEONE IN NEED.

My "aha" moment came one day when I saw my salon completely filled with clients who were getting their haircuts and other services. Understanding the potential power that a large number of people could have, I realized that a business could be a powerful vehicle for philanthropic efforts if someone could simply harness the compassion that resides inside each of our clients and show them how to help out in their community. This realization brought about my decision to start including "giving programs" in our annual marketing plan.

Every month throughout the years, Studio 904 has given back to our community and to our world. Each "giving program" is designed to be a fun event. At the same time, we provide education and awareness about the importance of supporting those who are silently suffering. I am sincerely grateful that our clients enthusiastically supported our initial efforts and continue to do so today.

Over the past several years, some of our memorable community service projects have included: children's haircutting programs in low-income grade schools; haircuts for out-of-state parents staying at the Ronald McDonald House while their children received medical treatment at Seattle Children's Hospital; food drives to benefit the Northwest Harvest's food drive for children; help for the tsunami victims in Japan; donations to help national disaster victims in the U.S.; support for the Youth and Family Services organization; funding for animal advocacy nonprofit organizations; and many more.

15 ✂ TAKE ACTION TO CORRECT A WRONG.

I spent time with a local animal welfare organization, helping animals that were rescued from "puppy mills" in Washington State. It was heart-breaking to see the rescued dogs in the back of a large van as volunteers brought them to a parking lot where they were examined. Every dog was so scared and shaking that we had to entice them out of their crates with treats, love, and patience. I remember one little poodle dog's leg instantly breaking as he tried to step out of his kennel; he had not been outside of his kennel for the first two years of his life. One staff person told me that another sickly dog had deceased puppies inside her stomach that still needed to be removed. These dogs needed so much medical care before they were ready for adoption that I decided to hold a fundraiser in my salon. Over 100 people responded to my calls for help and we raised over $10,000 to assist with their medical bills. Although I still have painful memories from my time working with the dog rescue organization, it helped my healing process knowing that I and my compassionate clients and friends were able to do something positive to improve the lives of these animals.

"I am in favor of animal rights as well as human rights. That is the way of a whole human being."

— Abraham Lincoln

16 ✂ FIND AND SUPPORT A CAUSE THAT YOU FEEL CONNECTED TO.

Since helping dogs rescued from puppy mills, a huge animal fundraiser was added to our yearly list of giving programs for the months of November and December. To date, we have raised a large amount of money for various animal organizations in the state. The name of our giving program, "Angels for the Animals," was chosen because of a letter of appreciation I received from Pasado's Safe Haven, an animal rescue organization in Washington State. It read, "Kay, thank you from the animals. You are truly their Angel." I urge you to become an Angel for your chosen organization, too!

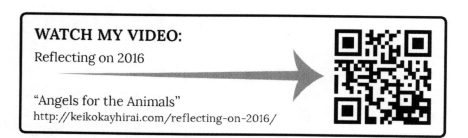

WATCH MY VIDEO:

Reflecting on 2016

"Angels for the Animals"
http://keikokayhirai.com/reflecting-on-2016/

MANY CULTURES, ONE TEAM

My sincere thanks and gratitude to those who have made this journey with me throughout the years. Without their caring guidance, strong support, and boundless energy, I would not have been able to realize my dream of building a unique salon that gives back to the community. There are too many to name, but I would like to introduce you to my current team at Studio 904 Mercer Island, as well as a few significant members who have helped along the way. Each person describes the path that he or she took to Studio 904 and how working at the salon has affected them personally and professionally. I think you will find their stories both interesting and inspiring.

"A ship in the ocean continues on its course if its engines are maintained by a skillful crew and the captain is focused on the direction of the journey..."

— Author Unknown

KAORU

What were you doing before you started working at Studio 904 and why did you choose to work there?

In the summer of 1999, I was looking through the classified ads in the Sunday newspaper. Studio 904 was advertising for a part-time bookkeeper. At the time, I was working as an office manager at a local hotel while attending my final year of college. I enjoyed working at the hotel, but I needed to reduce the number of work hours so that I could concentrate more on my studies. When I saw the ad, I thought it would be a good fit for me because I enjoyed interacting with people and I had bookkeeping experience. Most important, though, was the fact that the job had flexible hours.

On the day of my interview, I sat down with Naomi, the salon manager, and Kay, the owner, in the small back office of the salon. The first thing we talked about was how I should be addressed; I thought "Kaoru" might be too difficult to pronounce for a lot of people. Kay responded that it was a beautiful name and suggested that I use it because it represented the "real me." When I heard that comment, I was quite moved. I couldn't believe that Kay was not only offering me a job, but she was also acknowledging that I was a unique individual who could bring distinct skills and ideas to the salon.

What are the most important things that you have learned while working at Studio 904?

Early on, I realized that we are not only providing quality hair services, but we are also helping to instill confidence and self-esteem in our clients. I learned that there are many reasons people come to our hair salon. Foremost, their hair is generally too long and needs to be cut. Beyond that, however, are other motivations to make an appointment. Sometimes it is to change their look by choosing a different hairstyle. Other times, the salon provides a welcoming place to socialize and interact with our stylists. I learned that it is important to respond to each client's needs so that we can make their lives easier and put a smile on their face as they leave the salon.

As a business, I also believe it is important that we focus on a four-part strategy I call "Win-Win-Win-Win." First of all, we have to win with our clients. Second, we have to win with all of our employees. Third, we have to win at making our business successful. And, finally, we have to win by supporting our community. It is very challenging to balance this "winning" strategy because oftentimes there are forces that pull stronger in one direction than the other, forcing us to sacrifice one area over another. By striving to maintain a proper balance with all four areas, however, great harmony and positive outcomes can be achieved.

What do you like most about working at Studio 904?

I like the fact that everyone works as a team to ensure that the business is successful. Everyone has the opportunity to provide input and make decisions in order to move the salon forward. Because Studio 904 is a small business and many employees have worked here for a number of years, it feels like we are "family."

What is the most important thing that you would like clients to know about Studio 904 that they may not be aware of?

When I think of Studio 904, I think of the tremendous efforts we have made to support the local community. We donate our services to numerous local community organizations throughout the year. Over the past 17 years that I have been employed with Studio 904, there were many times when the business struggled. Even during those tough times, Kay never wavered in her support of the community. I can't remember the number of times that I warned her "We are not a charity organization, so we need to concentrate on making the business profitable." Although we sometimes have to make a few concessions, Kay's passion for giving back has been unrelenting. I now understand that supporting the community will only make our business stronger as we assist those who need a helping hand. It is very fulfilling to work for this kind of business.

Do you have any "memorable" moments that shaped how you now view the world and the people and events around you?

The friendly and supportive working environment at Studio 904 has made me treasure the friendships I have made. I also think that we have a great group of clients who also contribute to the positive energy in the salon. It has made me realize how lucky I am to be surrounded by people I sincerely care about.

Unfortunately, I unexpectedly lost both of my parents about four years ago. It was a very difficult time for me. Not only would I not see them anymore, but I had a lot of regrets about the "should haves" and "could haves" that did not take place. I often ask myself why didn't I visit them more often or simply call them when I had the chance? Sometimes, you never know the true value of a moment until it is only a memory. Life is unpredictable, so it is important to be grateful for every moment, focus on what matters most, and associate with the people who make you happy and bring enjoyment to your life.

TINA

What do you like most about working at Studio 904?

One of the most rewarding aspects of my job has been working with the salon's diverse group of clients. One individual in particular stands out in my mind. I met Mary while working at Kay's salon in Pioneer Square, Seattle. She came in regularly for a bob, a popular style that is cut one length with a slightly graduated neckline. One day, I suggested a "pixie," which is a very short, shaggy, and choppy cut, sensing that it would better suit her personality and career as a graphic designer. After I was finished, she loved the edgy, more avant-garde look. This kind of faith and trust that I receive from clients empowers me to believe in myself. It gives me the confidence and willingness to push for new ideas and suggestions instead of settling for the same approach or hair style on each client's visit.

The other thing that amazes me is that my clients are so forgiving. Recently, we switched to a new hair product line. This change required a reformulation of the hair color for a client named Paula. The eventual outcome was not good! I will forever remember her reaction to the bright red hair and her kind words to me afterwards. As she was laughing at the results, she said to me "Tina, you could make my hair purple and I would still come to you!" It was a very humbling experience. Since that particular moment in the salon, Paula and I have become close, personal friends.

What is the most important thing that you would like clients to know about Studio 904 that they may not be aware of?

There is a mutual respect and understanding that enables us to become our clients' confidant. We find ourselves being supportive, asking advice from one another, or just listening. The relationship of loyalty, trust, and appreciation comes about only through the time and experiences that are shared with them. Hair is a very personal and emotional expression of ourselves, so it is important to make our clients feel happy and satisfied with how they appear when we are finished. When they exit the salon, you want to feel like you have made a difference in not only their appearance, but in their total well-being.

MARIA

What inspired you to become a hair stylist?

At the ripe old age of sixteen, I already knew that I wanted to be a hair stylist. Nothing else seemed to matter in my life. For me, high school was boring and uninteresting, so I knew that I wanted to get on with my career as soon as possible. Fortunately, Mrs. Valentine, my school counselor, noticed how unhappy I was with my studies. At one of the quarterly parent-teacher conferences, she met with my mother and me and suggested that the "Bright Futures" program might be a good fit to explore some additional interests. The program allowed students to begin training for a job while continuing to earn high school credits in order to graduate. I quickly enrolled at the Seattle Vocational Institute and excelled in their course work, finishing a two-year program in just fifteen months. Eager to enter the "real world" to make a living, I was thrilled when I was finally able to obtain my hair stylist license.

How did you find yourself working at Studio 904?

My initial plan was to work at Super Cuts, a national chain of hair cutting salons. Mrs. Valentine, however, had other ideas for me. She had one last request before I left and insisted that I do a month-long internship at Studio 904. Of course, I was initially not interested and vehemently opposed her plan. She was very persistent, however, and even volunteered to accompany me to the interview. I finally gave in and I am so glad that I did.

What do you like most about working at Studio 904?

I love the work environment. After ten years, I am still working at Studio 904 and often think about how my life might have been so different if it were not for the encouragement that Mrs. Valentine provided. Over the years, I have heard some really ugly stories about the competition and dysfunctional environments at other salons – harsh realities that I fortunately didn't have to experience. My place at Studio 904 is somewhere I can thrive and feel completely comfortable and secure. I work with a team of individuals that is supportive, positive, and encouraging. Looking at it from that perspective, I feel very much like a success story!

ANTUAN

What inspired you to become a hair stylist?

As long as I can remember, I have enjoyed giving haircuts. When I was younger, I gave haircuts to my buddies in high school. I think what won me over was the enjoyment in seeing their transformations. Each of them came to me looking pretty shabby, but after I was done, they left looking like a brand new person! Soon after, I came to the realization that if I just learned a little bit more and developed my skills, this was probably something that I could do professionally.

What were you doing before you started working at Studio 904?

In search of fulfilling my goal to be a hair stylist, I traveled from South Carolina to Seattle. After I arrived, the first thing I did was to enroll in a program to be a barber. When I completed my studies, I was surprised, but pleased to know that I was prepared to cut hair on anyone - kids, teens, men, and women. I could hardly believe that I had achieved my objective and was now a fully-trained, professional hair stylist!

What do you like most about working at Studio 904?

Each morning when I arrive at work, I am cheerful, excited, and ready to meet whatever challenges my clients present to me; I act as their listener, consultant, and provider. The best moments are when I see the "Wow!" expressions on their faces. I am absolutely ecstatic when I bring that much joy and satisfaction to an individual. I love working at Studio 904 because I work with a supportive team that gives me the security and confidence to do a great job. The environment is nurturing because I learn new techniques every day and also have the opportunity to improve my problem-solving skills, time management, and consulting skills along with the other stylists. So far, it's been an incredible journey and one that I hope continues for a long time.

LINDA

What inspired you to choose this particular career?

A lot of my inspiration for doing this kind of work in the salon has definitely come from my mother, who worked as a nurse in Laos. Her energy and concern for others was boundless and empowering for me. Growing up in an environment where I constantly witnessed my mother's natural and professional ability to heal people made me recognize the potential power in the human hands. I feel I am an extension of my mother. Through my work as a hair stylist and aesthetician, I am healing and helping individuals just as my mother had done for so many years. I want to always embrace and be mindful of my skills and talent to benefit not only myself, but others as well.

What do you like most about working at Studio 904?

There is a lot of satisfaction that comes from working with our clients. A few years ago, at the end of a long day, Kay walked into the spa room and approached me. She said, "I just talked to Mary Ann, one of your clients. She wanted me to tell you that she was "in heaven" and thought that your hands were a true gift. Because your treatment always leaves her with such a personal "high," she said that she wishes she could start each day with what she called 'Linda's Touch'." After hearing those comments from a client, I couldn't stop smiling; it told me that something very special and magical occurred during our session. We were somehow able to share some positive energy that the both of us had created and, as a result, contributed to the other's exuberant mood! An experience like that is one of the things that I really enjoy about my job.

JACKIE

What were you doing before you started working at Studio 904?

While I was attending college, I decided to move from my home town in Honolulu, Hawaii to Centralia, Washington. After I arrived, I wanted to continue my studies at the local college. Unsure of what subjects I wanted to pursue in school, I decided to help out with my mother's cleaning business for a while. My stepfather, however, had other ideas about a career for me and suggested that I look into attending beauty school. After I completed my training, I eventually found my way to Studio 904.

What do you like most about working at Studio 904?

I was warmly welcomed the moment I stepped in the door and immediately liked working alongside the other team members. The concept of working as a team was not practiced at any other place I had previously worked. I felt important and accepted, but most of all, I felt valued because the team acknowledged that I had something worthwhile to contribute. That was twelve years ago. To this day, I continue to sharpen and improve my skills as a hair stylist, consultant, adviser, and acute listener.

What is the most important thing that you would like clients to know about Studio 904 that they may not be aware of?

A big benefit of working at Studio 904 is that our staff is like family. Many of our clients view us as extended members of their family.

Do you have any memorable moments at Studio 904 that have had an impact on how you view things now?

I clearly remember one client, named Nancy, who dropped by one day to tell us her son had passed away. That personal moment really stuck with me. It made me realize that many clients feel so comfortable with us that they want to share personal events – whether happy or sad, uplifting or tragic. I am truly blessed to be a part of the Studio 904 family because I am doing something meaningful with my life and something that feels truly "right" for me. It's a great feeling.

MIRIAM

What were you doing before you started working at Studio 904?

I obtained my stylist license through an apprenticeship program that was sponsored by Studio 904 and South Seattle Community College (SCCC). All of my practicum and training was performed at the salon, but I reported to SCCC once a week. This type of program wasn't for everyone, but I liked it a lot. It not only taught me self-discipline, but also encouraged me to learn independently.

While working at the salon, what kinds of things have you learned about yourself and about the business?

To date, I have worked with Kay and her staff for eleven years and the experience has really opened my eyes. I found that I love the creativeness that comes with the work and always try to do my best to meet my clients' needs. One of the frustrating things for me, however, is that I am sometimes limited as to how long I can spend with each client. Kay is very aware of how some of these time metrics get in the way and how frustrating it can be for a stylist when they want to always do their best. To her credit, though, she has gone out of her way to educate us about the basics of not only hair, but also about how good metrics matter in operating a successful business and keeping things running smoothly.

There may be a lot of glamour in owning your own salon, but I realize how much time and hard work Kay puts in as the owner. The expenses that are involved with wages, hair products, and marketing are incredible and the time she takes in training the staff is seemingly endless. Even as challenging as it is, Kay's philosophy of giving back to the community and those less fortunate is unyielding. I admire the commitment that she gives to her work with the salon, its employees, and the wider community. It makes me understand and see more clearly the dilemma between the art of creating beauty and maintaining a successful business.

SIMI

What were you doing before you started working at Studio 904?

I was born in Canada in a small area near the farmlands. Although my mom's family is Muslim and very religious, I did not spend much time studying religion when I was growing up. Instead, my mom encouraged me to choose my own path. As a result, I worked at a small Indian grocery store and also studied to earn my UX design certification.

What is your current role at Studio 904?

I am the salon coordinator and am also involved in handling the marketing of Studio 904 on social media.

What do you like about working at Studio 904?

Studio 904 has a very family-like environment. Everyone is very friendly and we all come from different cultures and backgrounds. Kay holds a lot of fundraisers and works with different charities, which I love getting involved with.

Before working at the salon, I was somewhat of an introvert and did not really talk to the people I worked with. Working at this salon, however, has taught me to open up to people. I have also learned how to handle many different situations at work. As a result, I have developed a sense of responsibility and have taken on a leadership role, two things that will stay with me forever.

TASSIE

How did you first find out about Studio 904?

I first met Kay when I was seventeen years old. At the time, she was working at a salon called Hair on Broadway, the first one she owned. I was introduced to her by my mother, Maryann Pember. At that age, how you look and feel about yourself is very important and how your hair looks is a large part of your image and self-esteem. Unfortunately, because of my young age, I wasn't able to find any salon that would listen to my concerns about how I wanted my hair to look. All of the stylists I had would always smile and nod and then do whatever they felt like. I cannot tell you the countless number of times I left a salon crying, telling myself that "it is only hair; it will always grow back."

What did you like about your initial experience at the salon?

The minute I walked into Hair on Broadway, I knew that things were going to be different as I was enthusiastically greeted by name as soon as I entered the salon. Then, my stylist came over to meet me, ushered me to a chair, and actually had a conversation with me before even washing my hair. We discussed what I wanted done, the pros and cons of my ideas, and how the finished style would look. This engaging experience continued to morph as I was introduced to another stylist who washed my hair and dried it. As she was doing that, she explained that I was getting a team of specialists to work with me and not just one person. Needless to say, I was thrilled at all of this attention. And, you can imagine the final results of my haircut. It was outstanding! However, this was not my last surprise of the day! As I left to pay, with a huge smile on my face, I tried to tip the multiple people who worked with me and was told: "No tips here. Your satisfaction is our tip." I was hooked.

What has your relationship with Studio 904 been like over the years?

My husband and I started a consulting company that works with small-to-medium-sized businesses. The companies we worked with were usually sole proprietorships, i.e., entrepreneurs that wanted to start working "on their business" rather than constantly working "in their business." We basically functioned in the role of a "CEO" for them. Kay learned about our company and asked us to help her. We developed a structural framework so that she could continue to build exciting programs for her business, staff, and the community.

During the next decade, I worked closely with Kay. Our company was hired to guide her salon, but I learned so much from her about running a business during our frequent meetings. For example, she taught me that learning is a lifelong journey, to be achieved in small incremental steps; you can have a profitable business and still give back to your community; and, finally, in an industry that is usually all about the individual "star stylist," you can create a team that works together and supports each other, rather than competes with one another.

It has been an honor to work with Kay and her team. Little did I know that one appointment would develop into a business relationship that has lasted over thirty-five years.

KRYSTAL

How has your upbringing impacted your life and work ethic?

My life's journey began in Vietnam. I still remember tremendous hardship and frightening experiences growing up. From the age of seven, my job was to haul heavy canned goods to my mother's store in a wheelbarrow that was twice my size. The most dreadful event, however, happened when I was nine; my family was forced to flee from Vietnam. We sailed for months in cramped and filthy conditions aboard a cargo ship. When we finally docked in Hong Kong, I was forced to jump from the sinking ship. The lessons that I learned during those formative years have impacted me throughout my life. Strength, endurance, persistence, responsibility, and hard work have been ingrained in me forever.

What were you doing prior to coming to work at Studio 904?

When I graduated from the cosmetology program at SCCC (Seattle Central Community College), I was eager and ambitious, immediately going to work as a hair stylist at Super Cuts. Within six months, I was promoted to the position of manager/hair stylist. I often worked ten hours a day, seven days a week. After working relentlessly for eight years, my shoulder muscles were permanently damaged, so I could no longer work as a hair stylist. Discouraged and exhausted, I took a year off to allow my body to heal. After evaluating my options, I returned to work and was a coordinator at another salon until it closed seven years later.

Everything I had done early in my career would not have been possible without the hard work and devotion of my mother-in-law; she was truly an inspiration. With her support and encouragement, my husband, Patrick, and I pursued our careers and started a family. I will never forget the boundless energy, care, and love she provided us so that we could fulfill our dreams.

What do you like most about Studio 904?

There are many reasons why Studio 904 is an exciting place to work. Besides styling hair, we have fundraisers, campaign rallies, and holiday events. And, because Kaizen (a philosophy for lifelong learning) is our mission, we are regularly exposed to new information and fresh ideas. Last, but certainly not least, Kay has provided opportunities to improve my personal growth in the areas of improving my communication skills, interacting with people, and running a business. These past thirteen years have been a pleasure for me and are much appreciated.

JANET

What were you doing before you came to Studio 904?

Previously, I had been working for a large salon chain. Life was very stressful there. All of the stylists were responsible for marketing themselves to bring in clients, which included handing out coupons on the streets of downtown Seattle. In addition, any products that were needed to service clients were charged to our accounts. Nothing was omitted; even stamps that I needed for mailers were deducted from my paycheck. In the end, there were hardly any earnings to take home.

How did you end up at Studio 904?

Craigslist led me to Studio 904. The team work concept and additional training attracted my attention when I read their ad. I went for an interview, talked to Kay and some of the other stylists, and immediately felt very comfortable with everyone I met that day. The most amazing part was that I would not have to worry about bringing in clients and buying my own products. Wow! I couldn't believe that everything was provided by the salon!

What has been the hardest thing for you while working at Studio 904?

Getting used to helping with other stylist's clients and then eventually taking some of them on as my own was the hardest thing for me. I knew that the clients were used to a certain high standard and having to maintain that was intimidating for me at first. Working as a team, however, helped me to gradually gain my confidence and develop a style that clients were open to and eventually willing to accept.

What is one thing that a client might be surprised to learn about Studio 904?

One of the nicest services that Studio 904 provides is that we keep track of the dates when clients come in for a cut, color, or spa treatment. Also, a stylist sometimes records information about a vacation, marriage, birthday, etc. This kind of data helps us provide more exact procedures at the proper time and with a personal touch. Clients are not always aware of all the record keeping that is going on behind the scenes to make their visit to our salon so efficient and pleasant.

What is your most memorable moment while working at Studio 904?

Even though I have been at Studio 904 for almost three years, I still remember the day when Kay handed me my first paycheck. I actually started to cry because I was so surprised and overcome with happiness when the salon owner took the time to meet with me. Kay sat me down and explained how I had earned my pay and how I could increase my earning potential as I advanced in my training and capabilities.

Why do you like working at Studio 904?

It is pretty obvious why I love working at Studio 904 so much. The people that I work with look out for my well-being in a healthy and nurturing environment. They are always willing to listen, provide advice, and respond promptly to my problems, concerns, or worries. In return, I feel that they greatly appreciate and value what I contribute to Studio 904 as a stylist and as a team member.

LILLY

What was your inspiration for joining the hair care industry?

When I was around six years old, I remember that my mother had a girlfriend named Terry. In those days, she was known as a "beautician." Terry and her husband, Yo, lived in Moses Lake and were childless. Together, my mother and Terry decided that it would be a nice break for me to get away from my three brothers and spend part of my summer vacation with Terry. She had a salon attached to her house and I would watch with amazement when she transformed plain-looking ladies into stunning and attractive women. When I saw that happen, I decided that that's what I wanted to be when I grew up!

As the years went by, however, I got sidetracked into other areas. I started a career as a "stewardess" (now known as a flight attendant) with the airlines. After a few years of flying, I got married and raised two children. Later, I continued working for the airlines in an administrative capacity. During my career with the airlines, I became very proficient in delivering excellent customer service to our customers, but did not even come close to fulfilling my childhood dream until I came to Studio 904.

What do you like about working at Studio 904?

While working at Studio 904, I discovered how rewarding it was to see clients looking and feeling so much better about themselves as they left the salon. I especially like seeing the transformation and their smiles. On a few occasions, I have had to deal with unhappy customers, which is always a challenge. My strong customer service training and skills, however, generally change the *unhappy* to *happy* by turning dissatisfied clients into lifelong clients.

The culture at Studio 904 is like attending a finishing school. I have witnessed stylists blossom into sophisticated, confident, and cultured professionals. When they work at the salon, they join not only a team, but a family. They regularly help and assist one another and share in each other's growth. Witnessing this transformation and personally being a part of it makes working at Studio 904 an enjoyable and FUN place to spend my time.

What are some of the things that clients may not know about Studio 904?

Many clients are not aware of Studio 904's philosophy of "The Continuous Improvement Process," i.e., learning and practicing Kaizen. This practice not only helps the employees at the salon, but also in our daily lives. I believe that our lives would be a lot less satisfying if we did not continually grow in spirit, mind, and body, so Kaizen reinforces and promotes the positive things in our lives.

Even though I am not living my childhood dream of being a stylist, I am proud to be employed at Studio 904 as an assistant salon coordinator. I have learned that the front desk is the hub of this business because everything starts and ends there. You have to be able to multitask and juggle several items at once, but the challenge of working with clients and staff within this unique business environment makes it challenging and rewarding at the same time. I am glad that I have the opportunity to be a part of this team.

DEBBIE

What made you decide to work at Studio 904 instead of other salons that wanted to hire you?

I chose to work at Studio 904 because it is a very unique salon. Kay, the owner, is very involved in community efforts and organizes several fundraising events each year to help make our world that much better. She is an example of a powerful business woman and she conscientiously promotes diversity in the workplace. After my job interview with her, I knew that Studio 904 was my kind of salon because I wanted to be a part of what Kay was doing for her salon family, its clients, and the local community. To witness and be a part of a small business that is making such a huge difference in people's lives and doing worthwhile things is just amazing and humbling to me.

What are the most important things that you have learned while working at Studio 904?

I have learned a lot of things, from customer service, to what teamwork is really about, to problem solving, and to finding the proper solutions. It is also important to be open to changes and to make something right when something doesn't turn out the way it was originally intended.

What do you like most about working at Studio 904?

I share the same basic philosophy as Kay, i.e., giving back to the community. Do what we can as individuals, whether it is helping animals, feeding children, or promoting a green environment. Also, I like the Kaizen philosophy that promotes continuous learning. Kay is a great teacher, a mentor, and a friend who has taught all of us to be lifelong learners and to improve as we grow in our various roles at the salon.

What is the most significant thing that you would like clients to know about Studio 904 that they may not be aware of?

Since 2005, Studio 904 has been my "home away from home." The salon feels so comfortable to me because it promotes giving back, helps create jobs, offers valuable life lessons, and builds strong team relationships.

Do you have any memorable moments and/or thoughts that have shaped your life philosophy?

I believe in building relationships and growing as an individual. One of the things that has always driven me is something that I heard at an early age: "The stimulus for the lobster to grow is when it starts to feel uncomfortable." What that means to me is that times of stress are also opportunities for growth. If we use adversity properly, we can actually grow. The questions that I frequently ask myself are: How can I make this better? How can I make a difference in our community and our world? How can one person possibly make a difference? I think the answer to those questions is pretty simple. Because we live in a fast-changing and growing society, we can't go about our ways by thinking only of ourselves and being selfish all the time. That is probably one of the reasons why volunteering has always been an important outlet to help me overcome hard times. Transitioning from a difficult childhood, to where I am now, I have learned to use any misfortunes that I have encountered to fuel my desire for positive growth. Having the opportunity to work with Kay and being a part of the Studio 904 family has made me extremely grateful for the inspiring role that they have played in my life.

ALEX

What were you doing before you met Kay and began working at Studio 904?

I was in my senior year at Seattle University. When I met Kay, I was taking a management course in the Albers School of Business.

What were your job responsibilities at Studio 904?

I started out as a salon coordinator at the Studio 904 Pioneer Square location. Afterwards, I transitioned to the salon manager position and worked at both the Pioneer Square and Mercer Island locations.

What were some of the important things you learned while working at the salons? Were there any life lessons?

There are many things that I attribute to my time at Studio 904:

- Adopting the concept of lifelong learning. Kay promotes the philosophy of "Kaizen," i.e., we should all be lifelong learners and we should strive for continuous improvement.

- Setting the stage and ambiance for our clients. Every morning, before the salon opened, we made sure that we were ready for our clients. It was more than just making sure that all of our equipment worked. It was going the extra step like running the hot water in the shampoo bowls so our first clients would not have to wait for the water to warm up before their shampoo. Fresh flowers from a local florist to hot apple cider in the winter months always added to the ambiance. She emphasized that "little things matter."

- Giving back. Studio 904 was very active in the local community, from giving 5% of product sales to a local charity, to providing haircuts to kids at First Place School, to participating as a salon in the Seattle Animal Shelter Furry 5K Fun Run and Walk. It was important to remember that we were part of a community and it was important that we all play a part in supporting our community.

- Caring for others. Studio 904 is a different type of salon, one that provides all of its staff reasonable wages, health and retirement benefits, and a team-oriented environment. This business strategy is different from most salons where stylists rent chairs, compete for clients, and wages fluctuate with the number of clients they see.

- Establishing a strong support network. While Kay was active in the day-to-day operations, she had the support of her entire family. Whether it was Tommy dropping off supplies, Sheri helping with birthday mailings, Ross designing new promotion material for the stations, or Lilly helping prepare for the holidays, it was a business that benefited from the strong support of Kay's family and friends.

What are you doing now?

I currently work in higher education in Illinois, developing and providing opportunities for students to continue their learning outside of the classroom through experiential learning.

NAOMI

How has your upbringing affected your approach to life and work?

I was born in Seattle to second generation Japanese-Americans who practiced Buddhism. At the age of six, I moved to Japan, attended a private, international, Catholic girls' school until the age of 15, and then returned to the United States. When I began high school in Bellevue, Washington, it was quite a culture shock because I had never attended a public school. After becoming assimilated in my new environment, I managed to make friends with a diverse group of students and was elected Junior Homecoming Princess, Laurel Guard, and cheerleader. I had some close friends who were Mormon, so I went on a trip to Salt Lake City to visit the Temple. Soon after, I realized that the religion was not for me and I decided to hold on to my Buddhist faith.

What did you like most about working for Studio 904? What was your role? What are some of the things you learned that have helped you navigate through your life's journey?

While working at Studio 904, I liked the Kaizen philosophy because the staff worked as a team instead of just as individuals. We not only improved our hair cutting/coloring/styling skills, but we also learned about running a business, becoming better people, and giving great customer service. Quality control and the apprenticeship program were some of the key projects that I worked on while I was there.

I started working at Hair on Broadway after finishing beauty school. After four years of working as a stylist, I had to leave because of complications from severe contact dermatitis on my hands. After working for an airline at Sea-Tac Airport for a few years, Kay asked me to return and work as a front desk coordinator at the Studio 904 on Pine Street. Over time, I became the salon coordinator and operations manager of both the Seattle and Mercer Island locations. When the Mercer Island salon ran into a few financial problems, I was asked to help stabilize the operations and bring it back to profitability. Here are some of the things I learned:

- Put systems that work in place.

- Don't change the people, change their actions.

- Never leave the house without some eyeliner or lipstick; you never know who you will run into at the store.

- You only get one chance to make a first impression.

Where are you living now and what are you doing to occupy your time?

I live in a small village in Switzerland with my husband and two sons, who are 14 and 12. There are only about 6,700 inhabitants in the surrounding area. My sons play soccer and participate in ski races. I help out at the soccer club's clubhouse restaurant in the spring and fall; during the winter, I work at a restaurant in a ski resort. I enjoy being able to be home when my kids come home from school or training.

There is a good quality of life in the Swiss Alps. I enjoy working in the service industry because I like interacting with the public. One of the things that still interests me is analyzing how businesses are run and finding ways that I can help make a business operate more efficiently.

MAI

Why did you choose to become a cosmetologist and where did you receive your training?

I was training to be a paralegal and also working for an auto insurance company. After a while, paralegal work didn't really seem that interesting to me. One day, I called my friend, who worked for a landscaping business. After we talked for a bit, he told me that he was attending a cosmetology school. It sounded exciting, so the next day I enrolled at the same school! When I spoke to my parents about my new career plan, they were really upset and told me that only people who didn't speak English worked in hair salons! In return, they didn't speak to me for three days!

What made you decide to work at Studio 904?

After becoming a licensed cosmetologist, I found a job opening at Studio 904 while looking through classified ads in The Seattle Times. The ad sounded interesting and promising, so I applied. When I arrived for my interview, I was surprised that it would be taking place in front of a camera crew, the salon stylists, and the salon owner. By chance, the camera crew was already there to do an interview with Kay for a piece on "The American Dream." My interview was accidentally scheduled at the same time. It was good timing, though, because I got the opportunity to listen to Kay's background and was really impressed to hear about her background and non-profit fundraising. All that said, I was so excited when I eventually found out that I had a job offer from Studio 904. Finally, I could look forward to building my skills in a challenging environment, as well as learn from Kay, whom I knew had so much to teach and offer.

What would some people be surprised to know about the salon industry?

The salon business is not as luxurious or glorified as some may think it is. There is a lot of behind the scenes work that goes on that most of our clients are probably not aware of. On the upside, though, there were definite benefits. I had some of the best clientele around, who were so interesting and fun to talk with; a super supportive group of teammates whom I wouldn't have traded for anything; and the type of work that allowed me to keep in touch with my creative side.

What did you like most about working at Studio 904?

The thing I liked most about working at 904 is the fact that all of us worked as a team. We worked for each other, not against each other. There was an honest desire for each stylist to help one another because we wanted everyone to succeed. I also loved our clients because they were so diverse and provided fascinating conversation. Some of my friends thought that cutting hair would be stressful, but I found that it was just the opposite because people were so open and you learned so many things in the process.

What is the one thing that you want Studio 904 clients to know?

I think Studio 904 clients should know that the stylists exist because of their support. Sure, we got paid, but if they didn't make the decision to have their hair services done at our salon, we were no longer needed. Most of the stylists like to work in this profession because they are a "people person," have a real passion for the job, and like the creative side of the business.

Is there one big takeaway that you learned while working at Studio 904?

For most people, life offers many different roads to take during their lifetime. It is up to the individual to decide whether to take one path or another. I have decided to face the major decisions in my life while I am still young and open to change versus when I am older and more apt to fight change. As I stated before, I like challenges and I am willing to work hard to achieve my goals. At the same time, it is great to know that I have a marketable skill and a backup career in the salon business if I choose to try another career and things don't work out.

BESSY

Please tell me a little bit about your background.

I was born and raised in El Salvador, but never knew my mother. Because my father had immigrated to the United States, I ended up living with my grandfather. Living in a small village was a struggle and did not offer many opportunities. When I was sixteen, I became pregnant and gave birth to my son, Kevin. Soon after, my grandfather contacted my father and asked if my son and I could live with him. My father agreed. Although my grandfather was sad to see us leave, he told me that it was the right thing to do because he wanted a better life for both of us.

What happened after you arrived in the United States?

I wound up in Seattle and got my green card shortly thereafter. Because I was a single mother, I knew that I had to get a job right away so I could live independently.

A friend told me about El Centro de la Raza, an organization that provides aid to Hispanic people in the area. I contacted them and they gave me assistance in learning English, which was a tremendous help, because I was eventually able to enter a cosmetology program at South Seattle Community College. While I was studying there, the school counselor told me about Kay and her efforts to help train immigrant women so that they could succeed in the cosmetology industry.

What are the most important things you learned while working at Studio 904?

I feel so much gratitude that Kay took me under her wings and patiently worked to improve my English and hair cutting skills. Most important of all, she taught me how to keep learning and growing for the rest of my life. I worked at Studio 904 for eighteen years. Because I didn't have any real role models or much parental guidance while growing up, I am grateful that Kay helped me to overcome some of the obstacles that I faced after coming to the United States.

What kind of work are you doing now?

I am now working as a medical assistant at Kaiser Permanente. While working at Studio 904, Kay provided me with a flexible work schedule so that I could study for an AA degree at Renton Technical College.

What kind of impact has Studio 904 had on your life?

It has been a long and difficult journey to get to where I am today. I am now married and have three wonderful children – Kevin, Kayla, and Karla. People at work often ask me, "Bessy, we are amazed at your work ethic. You treat our patients with kindness and respect. Where did you learn to do that?" I proudly answer, "I learned it while working at Studio 904."

JUSTIN

What were you doing before you started working at Studio 904?

I was working in the area of healthcare administration in Washington, D.C. and in Seattle for several years. That was followed by a brief stint working as a supervisor for Starbucks. As far back as high school, one of the things that I always wanted to do was become a hairdresser. My family and high school guidance counselors, however, discouraged me from entering that field. Once I moved away from my family, it was easier for me to finally make a decision to pursue a career in hairdressing. My husband knew that I wanted to find an outlet for my creative energies. He was also aware that I had always wanted to become a hairdresser, so he encouraged me to start researching cosmetology schools. After visiting a few of them, I was still not convinced that it was the right environment for me. Fortunately, Kay sat on the board of the organization that my husband worked for; he arranged for us to meet so I could pick her brain about the nature of the industry. At the time, Kay had just developed a pilot cosmetology apprenticeship program for the state of Washington. She explained the process and the program to me and I was immediately sold! I proceeded to interview for a place in the program and was subsequently accepted. The training was intense, but the entire staff was very supportive and helped me to learn the trade. Now that my creative urge was fulfilled, I surprisingly found that I was also comfortable working in the type of professional environment that Studio 904 offered. Unfortunately, their business model is a rarity in the industry.

What are the most important things that you learned while working at Studio 904?

The most important, ongoing life lesson that I learned at Studio 904 is that "It's not all about you!" I learned we all have to be open to life-long learning with ourselves, others, and the world around us. Just when we think we have it all figured out, we really don't. Keep searching, growing, and learning! Halfway through completing my studies for a bachelor's degree in communications, I am really grateful that the seeds that were planted during my time at Studio 904 have grown and given me the confidence to take on the next steps in my journey.

What did you like most about working at Studio 904?

I would have to say that my favorite thing about working at Studio 904 was the team that surrounded me; they were like a family. When you are working so closely with your co-workers day in and day out, seeing them at their best and at their worst, it is hard not to develop a bond. The Studio 904 family is somewhat unique because it is so diverse in terms of age, background, religion, race, ethnicity, and sexual orientation. I believe that this diversity is the strength that enables their team environment to thrive.

What is the most important thing that you would like clients to know about Studio 904 that they may not be aware of?

Clients would be interested to know, but hardly surprised, that Studio 904 is not just about styling hair. Obviously, this is a salon, and, it is a business. Working there, however, is about so much more. It is about challenging yourself and growing as an individual. And, it is about building professionalism, self-confidence, and a future that is bigger than just cutting hair while standing behind the chair. Kay also made sure that we learned the importance of caring, not only for our clients, but the community as well. During my time at the salon, we volunteered with the First Place School and Pasado's Safe Haven. When I wanted to add a pet to my family, I immediately thought of Kay and what she would say about supporting an animal shelter. And I did! Two cats later!

Do you have any memorable moments at Studio 904 that shaped how you view things now?

One "aha" moment that still sticks with me was a conversation between Kay, Tassie Christopher (our human resources consultant), and myself. I can't quite recall what I was frustrated about, but it had something to do with how I perceived my co-workers reacting to a conflict I was involved in. Tassie explained to me that when we put ourselves out there and gain the respect of others, we are then held to a certain standard - a higher standard. Because no one is perfect, we have to be aware of how we react to different situations. Additionally, when we position ourselves as a leader, it can often be a lonely place and we have to be prepared for more scrutiny. As everyone has these types of moments in their personal and professional lives, I still consider that as one of my top takeaways. It seems so simple, but it is so hard to internalize.

ACKNOWLEDGEMENTS

So much love and effort was poured into this book. For the past year, getting up at 6:00 a.m. each morning and going straight to my computer to write another chapter before heading off to work kept me on a pretty rigorous schedule. What motivated me to keep going was the desire to share my story and the lessons I learned so that others would be inspired to live their lives with passion. I wouldn't have been able to do it without such an amazing team who was there for me every day.

Randy Tada

My deepest gratitude for your patience and guidance. Always responding to my "red flag" messages crying "HELP!" Having you as my chief editor and coach taught me the importance of doing proper research and fine-tuning everything that is in my book. Your demand for quality is amazing and you've held me to the highest standards. Thank you also for enlisting your sister, Wendy, to help with the final review and editing of my book. The two of you together are a great team!

Maiya Gessling

I am honored that you read my first drafts and brought your creative and youthful energy to help my writing take on its own personality. You did your work from Okinawa, Japan, in spite of your busy schedule. Enjoy your adventurous life. You have a great literary future ahead of you.

Tamara Monosoff

I took your online class, "Author to Income," and I immediately felt a connection with you. Your professionalism and passion for guiding authors to integrate social media technology into publishing and promotion is what I needed. You helped me transform my book from ordinary to extraordinary.

Jean Nishi

Your thoughtful and kind interview skills helped everyone feel comfortable and safe in telling their stories. Thank you for capturing the essence of the people who worked for Studio 904. You are the most wonderful friend that anyone could ask for.

Tommy Hirai (My husband)

You are a wonderful husband, but more than that, you are my partner in life. We've shared the responsibility of raising a wonderful son and our beautiful injured daughter who will always need our help. You have helped me by doing everything you could to make sure that Studio 904 succeeded. Thank you for taking over the walking responsibilities of our feisty terrier dog, Max, and giving me the freedom to develop my business, write my books, and practice my artwork.

Ross Hirai (My son)

You helped me by creating "top notch" marketing designs and products that were so ahead of their time. I always remember you telling me, "Don't make it obvious, for example, by sending out Christmas mailers in colors of red and green. Get out of the box and design something different." You are one of the finest designers I know. You always come up with designs that prompt me to say, "This is exactly what I would have done if I had the talent to design."

Sheri Hirai (My daughter)

You have struggled since you sustained a head injury at the tender age of nine. The treatment you received from ignorant supervisors who had little understanding of persons with disabilities was painful for me to watch. Your determination to gain sustainable employment while pushing these obstacles to the side empowered me. It is because of you that I made a commitment to build a workplace that values diversity – a place where people from all walks of life are given the opportunity to grow and blossom in their chosen careers.

To all who have worked for Studio 904

I'm not sure you realize how important you have been in the development of this unique business. You have added life, energy, and hope for what we stand for. Every time I step through the front door of the salon, I feel like I've entered an oasis, away from the chaotic world outside. I am so grateful to have had the privilege to watch all of you emerge from cocoons and develop into beautiful butterflies!

To our wonderful clients

You've been there all along to support us through good times and bad. Even when we sometimes failed to deliver a perfect result for your hair services, you never gave up on us. You supported us through hundreds of fund-raising events and community outreach programs and mentored many of our stylists along the way. Several of you traveled with me on my entire journey – from the opening of my first salon, Hair on Broadway, to my present salon, "Studio 904 Mercer Island." Many years ago, I wrote this objective on a sheet of paper: "My goal is not only to have qualified employees, I want qualified clients." You have helped me to fulfill my dreams.

Last but not least

My heartfelt thanks to **Lila and Joe Greengard**. You have walked alongside of me since the early days of my business and have always been there when I stumbled and fell. Your gracious ways have taught me that it is not necessary to be an aggressive and single-minded business owner; instead, one can be kind, compassionate, and humble, and still succeed. Joe, you taught me an important lesson: "When what appears to be a giant 'paper tiger' blocking my way, it can always be gently pushed aside to clear the way." With you by my side, the tiger was never as frightening. I feel so fortunate that you decided to take me under your wing and share your wisdom.

KEIKO KAY HIRAI

Kay was born in Japan to a U.S. citizen, but because governmental regulations required her to return to the United States at the age of eleven in order to maintain her citizenship, she got a late start in the American school system. Entering her grade school as a fifth-grader, she did not know a word of English. After being a student who excelled in the Japanese school system, it was a humiliating experience for her. Most of her early school years were spent struggling to learn the English language and taking care of her ailing mother.

After finishing high school, she enrolled in a trade school to study cosmetology. However, she did not stop there. As a lifelong learner, she used the discipline and excellent study habits she developed in Japan to continue her education in any way that she could. She received on-going education from the University of Washington's Continuing Education Courses, community college classes, entrepreneurial programs, and various government courses offered by the Small Business Administration.

Kay Hirai opened her first salon business, named Hair on Broadway, in 1976. Now known as Studio 904 Mercer Island, the salon is recognized as an innovative small business. With twenty-five employees, it has become nationally known for its hiring practices, workforce training, economic development, and community outreach programs.

Hirai's passion and vision for "making the world a better place" and her ability to work collaboratively with public and private sectors made her the choice to chair the Governor's Small Business Improvement Council from 1997 to 2001. During this time, Kay traveled to Washington, D.C. as the state's delegate to participate in President Clinton's White House Conference on Small Business.

In 2003, she represented the small business and workforce training position in the Governor's Economic Development Commission under Governor Gary Locke. Hirai authored a "Direct Entry to Work" bill in the 2003 legislative session. It was successfully passed and was forwarded to Governor Christine Gregoire's office for her signature in 2008.

Hirai's innovative business model practices have also been recognized internationally. As a result, Studio 904 has been the recipient of numerous awards. In 2002, it became the first small business in the western region to win the "Better Business Bureau's International Torch Award for Marketplace Ethics" and in 2004, she was named the "National Minority Entrepreneur of the Year" by the U.S. Department of Commerce.

AWARDS AND HONORS

- 2015 Philanthropy Award (Mercer Island Youth and Family Services)

- 2011 Women of Courage Award (University of Washington's Women's Center)

- 2011 Best Business Award (Mercer Island Chamber of Commerce)

- 2010 Named as Nation's Model for a Flexible Workplace by the U.S. Women's Bureau

- 2006 Asian Entrepreneur "Innovation" Award

- 2004 Minority Entrepreneur of the Year Award (U.S. Department of Commerce)

- 2004 Finalist: Nellie Cashman Award

- 2002 Heart of Pioneer Square Award

- 2002 Better Business Bureau International Award for Marketplace Ethics

- 2001 Oregon and Western Washington Better Business Bureau Award

- 1999 National Philanthropy Award

- 1997 SBA Hero Award

- 1997 Washington State Quality Award, Certificate of Merit

- 1996 The Pacific Northwest Good Works Award

- 1995 Governor's Award for Workforce Training

- 1994 National Blue Chip Enterprise Award

- 1992 Mayor's Small Business Award

BOOKS THAT INSPIRED ME

Jacob's Journey: Wisdom to Find the Way; Strength to Carry On
Author: Noah benShea
http://keikokayhirai.com/books-that-inspired-me/

Business as Unusual: The Triumph of Anita Roddick
Author: Anita Roddick
http://keikokayhirai.com/books-that-inspired-me/

The Essential Deming: Leadership Principles from the Father of Quality
Author: W. Edwards Deming
http://keikokayhirai.com/books-that-inspired-me/

The E-Myth Revisited: Why Most Small Businesses Don't Work and What to Do About It
Author: Michael E. Gerber
http://keikokayhirai.com/books-that-inspired-me/

No-Compromise Leadership: A Higher Standard of Leadership Thinking and Behavior
Author: Neil Ducoff
http://keikokayhirai.com/books-that-inspired-me/

One Small Step Can Change Your Life: The Kaizen Way
Author: Robert Maurer, Ph. D.
http://keikokayhirai.com/books-that-inspired-me/

OTHER BOOKS BY KEIKO KAY HIRAI

Keiko's Journey

A compelling story about a young girl's life-changing experiences while growing up in postwar Japan.

Published by Chin Music Press - 2016

http://keikokayhirai.com/books-2/

Yumi's Life Lessons

*How to Empower Yourself and Turn Every Day
Into a Happy Day*

Second Edition: Published by Chin Music Press - 2016

http://keikokayhirai.com/books-2/

PHOTO CREDIT

Front Cover: Jamie Lynn Purnell
http://www.imagesbyjamielynn.com

49058972R00166

Made in the USA
San Bernardino, CA
11 May 2017